# Snake Charm

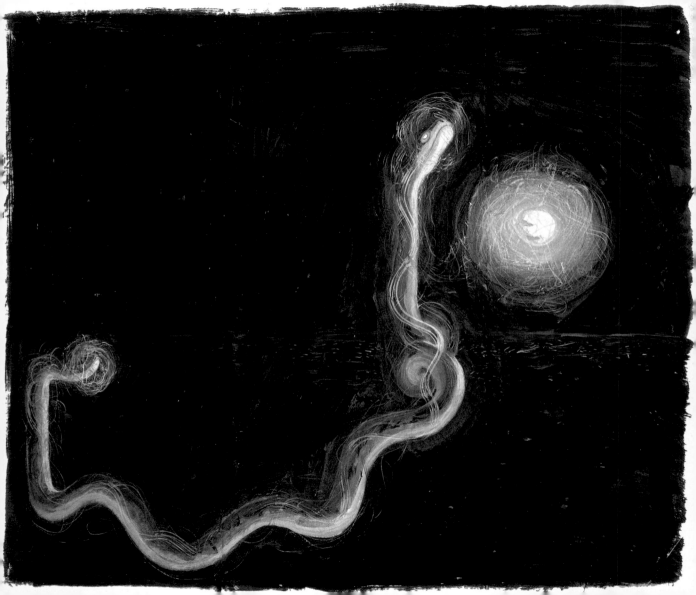

# Snake Charm

By Marilyn Nissenson and Susan Jonas

Harry N. Abrams, Inc., Publishers

For Ralph Esmerian, who suggested the idea for this book and whose generosity of spirit helped give it life

EDITOR: HARRIET WHELCHEL

DESIGNER: CAROL ROBSON

SUPPLEMENTARY PHOTO RESEARCH: BARBARA LYONS

Page 1: *Double-headed serpent pectoral. Mixtec-Aztec. Wood, covered with turquoise mosaic, with red and white shell, 7 x 16¾".* The British Museum, London;  Pages 2–3: *Morris Graves.* Snake and Moon. *1938–39. Gouache and watercolor on mulberry paper, 25½ x 30¼"; The Museum of Modern Art, New York. Purchase;*  Page 5: *Frederick Sandys.* Medusa. *1875. Black and red chalk on green paper, 28¾ x 22". By Courtesy of the Trustees of the Victoria & Albert Museum, London;*  Page 6: *Georges Fouquet. Winged serpent brooch. Chased gold, with champlevé and plique-à-jour enamel, with diamonds, emeralds, moss agate, freshwater and baroque pearls. 1902. Private collection;*  Page 7: *Franz von Stuck.* Sin. *c. 1912. Oil on canvas, 34½ x 20⅓".Villa Stuck, Munich;*  Pages 8–9: *Paolo Uccello.* Saint George Slaying the Dragon. *Oil on panel, 20⅙ x 35". Musée André Jacquemart, Paris;*  Page 10: *Michelangelo Buonarroti.* Cleopatra. *1534. Black pencil, 9 x 7". Casa Buonarroti, Florence;*  Page 11: *Sacrifice ceremony vessel. Moche, North Coast, Peru. c.* AD *200–800 . Painted ceramic, 11" high. American Museum of Natural History, New York;*  Page 12: *Kitagawa Utamaro.* Rat Snake. *From* Ehon mushi erabi *(Picture Book of Selected Insects), left half of plate 10. 1788. Woodblock print with colors on paper, 10½ x 7¼". The Metropolitan Museum of Art, New York. Rogers Fund, 1918;*  Page 13: *Albrecht Dürer.* Adam and Eve. *1507. Oil on wood, each panel 82¼ "x 31⅞". The Prado, Madrid;*  Page 14: *Elias van der Broeck.* A Still Life with a Snake Threatening a Lizard by a Clump of Toadstools, a Snail and a Butterfly Nearby. *Late seventeenth–early eighteenth century. Oil on panel, 8 x 10½". Courtesy Bob P. Haboldt & Co., New York;*  Page 15: *René Lalique.* Flacon. *1898–99. Agate and silver, 2½" high. Musée des Arts Décoratifs, Paris. Gift of Henri Vever, 1924;*  Page 16: *Michelangelo da Caravaggio.* Madonna and Child with St. Anne. *c. 1605. Oil on canvas, 9'7"x 6'11⅛".The Borghese Gallery, Rome;*  Page 17: The Virgin Tota Pulchra. *Mexican. Mid-nineteenth century. Painted tin, 10 x 7¾" The Girard Foundation Collection, Museum of International Folk Art, A unit of the Museum of New Mexico, Sante Fe*

Library of Congress Cataloging-in-Publication Data

Nissenson, Marilyn, 1939–
    Snake charm / by Marilyn Nissenson and Susan Jonas.
      p.    cm.
    Includes bibliographical references and index.
    ISBN 0–8109–4456–1
    1. Snakes—Folklore.  2. Serpents—Folklore.  3. Serpents in art.
  4. Serpents—Mythology.  I. Jonas, Susan.  II. Title.
  GR740.N57  1995
    398.24 ' 52796—dc20                                    94–42669

Published in 1995 by Harry N. Abrams, Incorporated, New York
A Times Mirror Company

Printed and bound in Hong Kong

# Contents

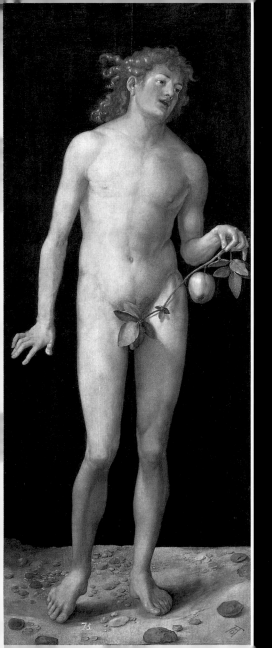

# INTRODUCTION

The snake insinuated itself into human consciousness at the beginning of time. Snakes are among our earliest gods. They were believed to mediate between life and death, earth and sky, this world and the next. They were consulted as oracles. They protected households. But snakes have been reviled as much as they have been revered. Snakes are symbols of seduction and betrayal, omens of disease and death. They have the power to kill, with venomous fangs or constricting coils.

Snakes inspire an atavistic hatred. They are more loathed than bats, maggots, or worms. Snakes slither. They are silent. They come and go without warning. They look slimy. Snakes have no differentiated body parts—no neck or limbs. Their eyes never close, and their expressions do not change. They are cold-blooded. They have a forked tongue. Baby snakes have no charm; they look like their parents, only smaller. Snakes are hard to anthropomorphize. They are mysterious, remote—the Other.

Snakes crawl on the earth—a permanently debased condition. They are associated with the dank, moldy floor of the forest. They lurk in tall grass and strike without warning; they drop from trees and squeeze their victims to death before swallowing them whole. Some people who are phobic about snakes faint at the mention of them.

People are willing to believe almost anything about snakes. The Roman chronicler Pliny the Elder was renowned in his day for his wide-ranging knowledge of the natural sciences, yet he gave credence to the most bizarre tales about snakes. In his *Natural History,* published in AD 77, Pliny described the enmity between snakes and elephants. The biggest elephants as well as the biggest snakes live in India, he reported, and they fight continually:

> Elephants are very cold blooded, and consequently in very hot weather are especially sought after by the snakes . . . [who] submerge themselves in rivers and lie in wait for the elephants when drinking. Rising up, [they] coil round the trunk and imprint a bite inside the ear, because that place only cannot be protected by the trunk. The snakes are so large that they can hold the whole of an elephant's blood, and so they drink the elephants dry, and these when drained collapse in a heap and the serpents being intoxicated are crushed by them and die with them.

*Relief from tomb at Chrysapha, Sparta. Sixth century BC. Staatliche Museen, Berlin*

*"Serpent Renewing Youth." From the Ashmole 1511 Manuscript, folio 84r. English. Bodleian Library, Oxford University*

Since prehistoric times, snakes have stimulated fantasies and inspired artists in all cultures. They have invaded our dreams. More cults have been devoted to snakes than any other animal. Serpents were worshiped in the ancient Middle East, around the Mediterranean basin, in China, and in India. They were sacred to the Norse, the Aztecs, the Mound Builders of Ohio, and tribal kingdoms on the west coast of Africa. When Greek and Mayan priest/astronomers studied the night sky, they saw serpents among the constellations and watched for their annual appearance as harbingers of the changing seasons.

Ancient societies ascribed astonishing power to snakes. Snakes were considered the wisest of animals; their unblinking eyes enabled them to see everything. The Bible describes the serpent that introduced Adam and Eve to the knowledge of good and evil as "subtle." In a Dahomey creation myth, the first humans were blind until a python god of wisdom opened their eyes to knowledge of the world.

To observers in the ancient world, snakes seemed to be immortal: resting in the shade, they appeared moribund, yet they revived miraculously in the warming sun; they shed their skin whole each year and emerged renewed. For many cultures—from the Indian subcontinent to the Mediterranean basin—a coiled snake came to symbolize the navel of the universe; one swallowing its own tail represented the endless cycle of life and death. Throughout the world, snakes reminded people of the inevitability of death and the hope of rebirth.

In the oldest myths, snakes were associated with the mother goddess. The earliest Egyptian symbol for goddess was a cobra. Early snake goddesses were propitiated in rites to ensure fertility and abundant crops. As an attribute of all-powerful mother goddesses like the Hindu Kali, the Greek Demeter, and the Aztec Coatlicue, the snake played a role in the growth and decay of vegetation, the beginning and the end of human lives.

Snakes had phallic power as well. In Vedic mythology, the cosmic serpent churned the primordial ocean to create the universe. Zeus, the supreme Greek deity, was once worshiped as a snake. In that form, he fathered Dionysus—god of orgiastic rites. Alexander the Great claimed direct descent from Zeus manifested as a serpent. The python was sacred to Apollo. Asclepius, the god of healing, took as his totem the caduceus—a snake twined around a staff or a tree trunk.

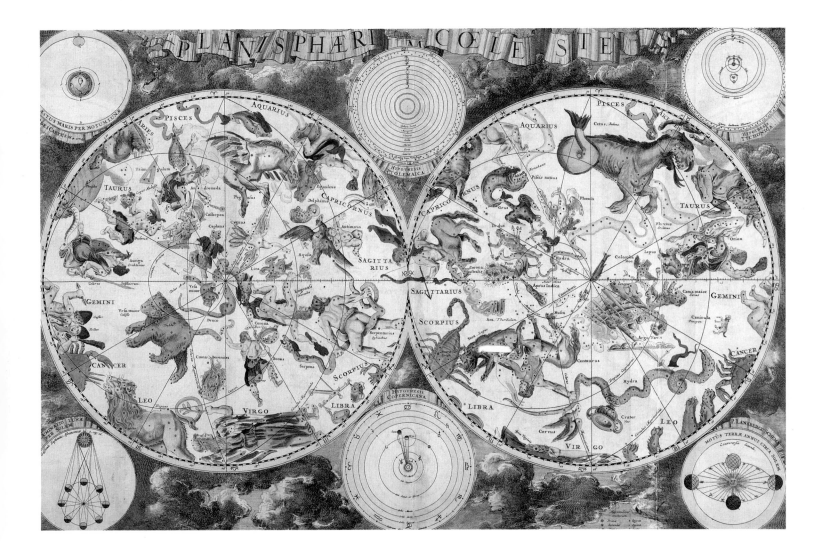

*Frederick de Wit.* Planisphaeri Coeleste. *1680. Courtesy Jonathan Potter Ltd., London*

De Wit's map of the heavens shows the Northern and Southern Hemispheres with traditional representations of the signs of the zodiac and constellations, including Draco, Serpens, and Hydra.

*Mosaic pavement. Italian. Twelfth century.*
*S. Demetrio Corone, Cosenza, Italy*

*Fresco. First century BC. Il Lararium.
Casa dei Vettii, Pompeii*

Egyptians interpreted the presence of benign snakes in their living quarters as a sign that the household was under the protection of benevolent spirits. Each neighborhood of the ancient city that would become Cairo had a shrine to a local snake/protector. Romans, too, believed snakes brought good luck. They wore amulets of carved snakes; shrines dedicated to snakes protected their homes and public places. Among the ruins of Pompeii, serpents painted on villa walls signify that the site was well guarded. According to Cicero and Livy, the appearance of snakes was a good omen, and their disappearance presaged disaster or death.

*William Blake.* The Temptation and Fall of Eve, *from Paradise Lost, 1808. Watercolor with pen, 19⅜ x 15¼". Courtesy, Museum of Fine Arts, Boston. Gift by Subscription*

Blake created a series of drawings to illustrate his interpretation of events described in John Milton's *Paradise Lost,* although the illustrations were never published formally together with the text.

The connection between snakes and good fortune continued during the Middle Ages and beyond. According to legend, King Arthur's ensign displayed an upraised serpent; subsequent rulers of England, claiming descent from Arthur, preserve a dragon on their coat of arms. During the First Crusade, Otho, the founder of the Sforza-Visconti dynasty, killed a Saracen warrior whose shield bore the device of a crowned snake swallowing a child. Otho's descendants, who ruled Milan for four hundred years, flaunted the crowned serpent as their family emblem.

Even though snakes were sometimes acknowledged to have protective power, they were generally shunned by Jews, Christians, and Muslims because they were blamed for the Fall of Man. After the snake tempted Eve to eat the forbidden fruit, he incurred God's punishment: "Because thou hast done this, thou are cursed above all cattle, and above every beast of the field; upon thy belly shalt thou go and dust shalt thou eat all the days of thy life" (Genesis 3:14).

Eve was assumed to be the snake's collaborator. According to some interpreters, Eve was related to the Semitic fertility goddesses Astarte, Ishtar, and Anat, all of whom were associated with snakes. (The Hebrew name for Eve—hawwah—is similar to the Aramaic word for snake—hiwya.) In their zeal to establish the cult of a single patriarchal deity, the writers of the Bible condemned all vestiges of religious practices associated with fertility.

Although Genesis does not identify the serpent with Satan, the early Church fathers blamed the snake for introducing evil and death into the world. The phallic serpent remained a potent symbol of wickedness throughout the Judeo-Christian and Muslim worlds for more than a thousand years.

During the Middle Ages, artists based their ideas about snakes on the Bible, although biblical writers were notoriously imprecise about animals in general. Snakes are mentioned thirty-five times in the Old Testament; sometimes the species can be identified, but more often the reference is vague or clearly fantastic, like the "fiery flying serpent" born of a cockatrice mentioned in Isaiah 14:29.

During the Renaissance, scholars and artists began to look at nature without theological preconceptions. Natural philosophers studied accounts of exotic wildlife by European explorers of Africa, the New World, and the Pacific and

*Banner of Massimiliano Sforza. Italian. Sixteenth century. From the* Fahnenbuch von Pierre Crolot. *Archives de l'Etat de Fribourg, Switzerland*

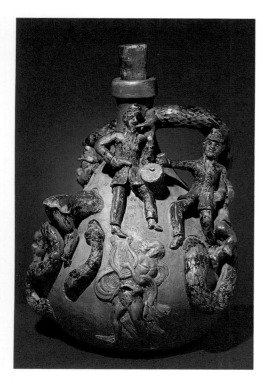

*Wallace Kirkpatrick. Civil War jug, Anna, Illinois. 1862. Incised, sculptured, polychrome-decorated salt-glazed stoneware, 10⅜" high. Collection of Fred and Kathryn Giampietro*

Kirkpatrick collected and exhibited live snakes. He also utilized them as a metaphor for evil on several jugs, which he designed to highlight the evils of drink and its association with political corruption.

began to examine and classify domestic flora and fauna. In the mid-sixteenth century, Conrad Gesner, a Swiss naturalist, published a monumental work entitled *Historia Animalium*. Gesner brought together everything that Greek, Roman, Arab, and medieval scholars had written about animals and added new information and detailed illustrations by the leading naturalists of his day. Gesner's work is a marvelous encapsulation of that moment when medieval and Renaissance beliefs existed side by side. The *Historia* included anatomically correct drawings of European snakes based on observation, as well as woodcuts of seven-headed hydras that supposedly lived beyond the seas.

An English curate named Edward Topsell incorporated many of Gesner's ideas and illustrations in his own multivolume *History of Four-Footed Beasts, Serpents, and Insects,* first published in 1607–8. Topsell's attitude toward snakes was ambivalent. His introduction promised that the book would contain "their Divine, Natural, and Moral Descriptions, with their lively Figures, Names, Conditions, kinds, and Natures of all venomous Beasts: with their several poisons and Antidotes; their deep hatred to Mankind, and the Wonderful work of God in their Creation, and destruction."

In his text, Topsell recounts an illustrative tale about farmers attempting to burn down a corn rick infested with adders:

> The straw would take no fire, although they labored with all their wit and policy. At last, there appeared unto them at the top of the heap a huge great serpent, which lifting up his head spake with a man's voice to the countrymen, saying:
>
> "Cease to prosecute your device, for you shall not be able to accomplish our burning, for we were not bred by Nature, neither came we hither of our own accord, but were sent by God to take vengence on the Sins of Man."

After Gesner and Topsell, writers of natural history gradually discarded accounts of imaginary beasts and eliminated moral judgment from their works. Throughout the eighteenth and nineteenth centuries, European explorers of the Americas, India, and Africa provided detailed information about vipers, pythons, cobras, and constrictors—creatures that previously had been more the subject of

myths than of science. Naturalists like Mark Catesby and John James Audubon, whose intent was to depict animals as accurately as possible, documented their discoveries with drawings and watercolors of specimens observed on field trips or preserved and brought back to the studio. Engraved and printed in books, these images were popular with an audience avid for scientific information.

In the late nineteenth and early twentieth centuries, the snake, freed from its Edenic context, was exploited by painters, decorative artists, and jewelers for the sinuous shape of its body and the subtle coloration and texture of its skin. But even secularized representations of snakes hint at licentiousness and blasphemy. Primordial associations of snakes with sexuality, fertility, and death were revived by discoveries in archaeology, depth psychology, and comparative mythology. A revival of interest in the past led Italian goldsmiths to create modern versions of Hellenistic snake bangles. Painters of the Victorian era returned to classical themes such as the garden of the Hesperides, the death of Cleopatra, the tragedy of Medea, and the saga of Hercules, in which gods and mortals contend with the power of the snake.

The snake continues to evoke fear and fascination. The enduring mystery is why. How has this phlegmatic, reclusive creature imprinted itself as such an evocative symbol in the human psyche? Other reptiles, equally cold-blooded and scaly, escape enmity. Children adore dinosaurs. Turtles are pets. Even alligators and crocodiles, which may be feared, are not loathed with the same intensity with which snakes are. Perhaps we have inherited the instinct to avoid a creature that can kill without warning. Perhaps we retain the awe inspired by the ancient alliance between snakes and the elemental forces of life and death. Art, at its best, makes palpable our fascination with snakes, acknowledges their beauty, and keeps alive the mystery of their hold on us.

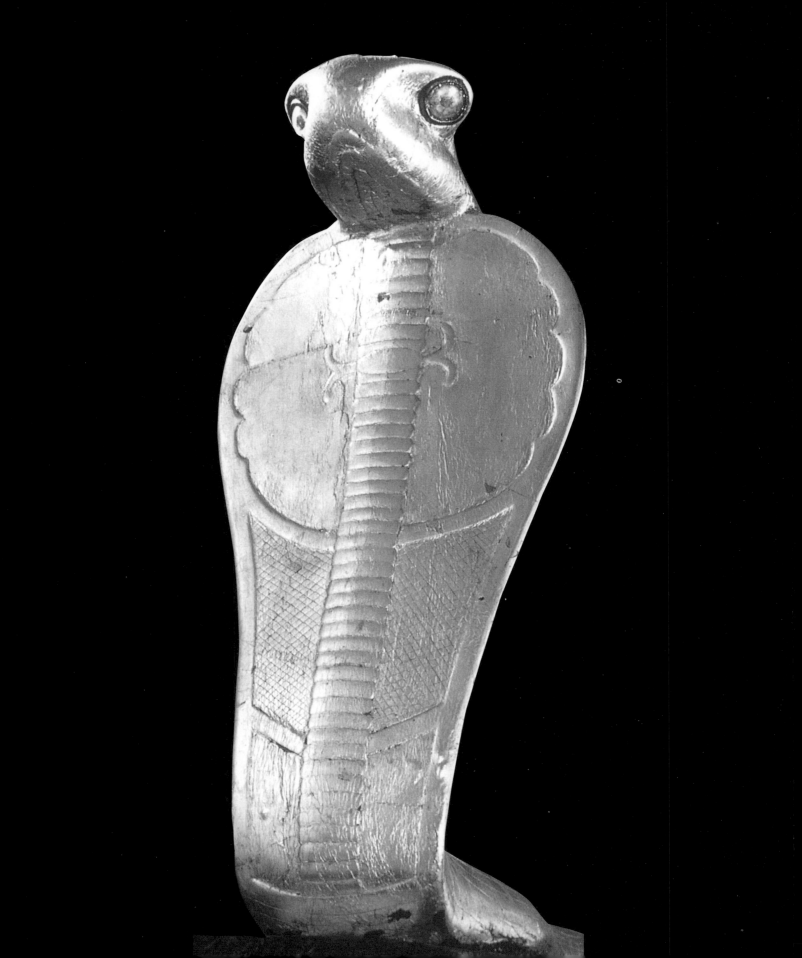

# DEITIES AND POWER

----------------------------------------

A thena, the patron deity of Athens, was worshiped at a shrine on the Acropolis after her cult spread from the island of Crete to the mainland. In classical Athens, her totem animal was an owl, which symbolized her wisdom, but Athena's Cretan ancestry was preserved in the little snake on her headdress and the presence of a resident snake at her shrine. In a monthly ritual, the priests of Athena offered a honeycake to the snake. During the Persian War at the beginning of the fifth century BC, the priests noticed that the snake refused to eat. This was taken as a sign that the goddess had withdrawn her protection from the city, which soon thereafter fell to the Persians.

Ancient people explained events as the work of a god or gods who controlled natural forces and intervened in human affairs. Often, particularly in the distant past, that god or goddess was a snake.

According to the myths of many cultures, a snake either created the universe or represented the chaos from which it emerged. The Egyptian cobra goddess, Neith, was the founder of the universe and the mother of the sun. Many heroes or gods, such as Marduk, Ra, Baal, or Zeus, killed a primordial snake-monster in order to assert their power. In other myths, snakes were symbols of chaos and order simultaneously. The *uroboros*—the immemorial image of a coiled serpent swallowing its own tail—has been interpreted as a representation of eternity and the endless cycle of annihilation and creation.

The universe was sometimes visualized as a tree with a serpent coiled around it. Shesha, a Hindu snake-deity, was also called Ananta (The Endless One) because he wrapped himself around the world. Yggdrasil, the Norse cosmic ash tree, was encircled by a serpent that protected and gnawed on it at the same time—a reminder that snakes embody the power of both life and death.

Snakes founded kingdoms and created cultures. The mythic progenitor of the first Chinese dynasty transformed himself into a snake; the first Han emperor was the son of a dragon. Several Greek city-states traced their origins to mythical kings whose names (like Erechtheus or Erichthonius) were variations of the combined root words for "snake" and "earth mother." Cadmus, the hero who killed a dragon and later took the form of a snake, founded the city of Thebes and gave its inhabitants the Phoenician alphabet. Quetzalcoatl,

*Golden cobra with dilated hood. Egyptian. c. 1325 BC. Gilded wood with translucent quartz eyes, painted at the back and set in copper or bronze sockets, 22½" high. Cairo Museum*

This wooden cobra represents a little-known Egyptian serpent deity named Netjer-ankh, which means the "living god." It was found in the innermost room of Tutankhamen's tomb. An inscription on the black pedestal describes the dead Pharaoh as "beloved of Netjer-ankh." Presumably Tutankhamen hoped the serpent would help him in his passage through the underworld.

*Stele of King Zet. Egyptian. c. 3000 BC. Limestone relief, 97½ x 25". The Louvre, Paris*

King Zet is known as the serpent king because of the serpent that serves as the hieroglyph of his name. The falcon, associated with the god Horus, indicates royalty.

the feathered serpent, was revered by the Maya as the inventor of their calendar and hieroglyphic script. In the grasslands of western Africa, the snake symbolized kingship; the periodic appearance of a snake at a king's village validated the ruler's claim to his throne.

The monsters who were challenged by the great heroes sometimes had many heads, which multiplied their malevolence. On the other hand, seven-headed snakes were symbols of good fortune. The seven-headed snake that supported and sheltered Buddha was like the cobra king who protected Vishnu, the Creator of the Universe in Hindu mythology.

The earliest astronomers considered seven a lucky number. Priests who studied the stars to predict recurring seasons, eclipses, and other heavenly phenomena, counted seven planets visible to the naked eye. They also calculated that seven was the midpoint in a thirteen-day lunar cycle and one of two factors in a twenty-eight-day lunar month. The number seven evolved as a portent of success, which it remains today. Seven signifies prosperity and fertility in classical Mexican numerology. The Japanese have seven gods of good luck. The seventh son is fortune's child; seven is a winner at the craps table.

Because snake gods had the power to mediate between life and death, order and chaos, and rainy and dry seasons, snake cult objects from the Americas and

*Wall painting. Egyptian. c. 2040–1080 BC. Magical scene from the tomb of Inkerka, Deir El Medina, Thebes, Egypt*

The rabbit is challenging the serpent, Apep, an incarnation of the sun-god, who appears to be guarding a sacred tree.

Asia were often portrayed with two heads, one at either end of the body. This mediating power could be schematized in a zigzag shape, which mimicked serpentine locomotion as well as a bolt of lightning; the association implied the ability to move back and forth between earth and sky. Heaven and earth were also bridged by rainbow-serpent deities common to many indigenous cultures in North and South America, as well as Australia.

Flying Chinese dragons had a similar dual nature. The feathered serpent is a motif of Amerindian art from the Mississippi Valley to the Isthmus of Panama. Quetzalcoatl, the most famous Mesoamerican serpent-god, began as a deity of earth and vegetation. As his cult was modified successively by the Toltec, Maya, and Aztec peoples, he acquired the green and golden feathers of the quetzal bird, which implied power in heaven as well as on earth.

Snakes represent the mother goddess in her procreative and destructive aspects. The Greek goddess Demeter and the Aztec Coatlicue were honored at corn festivals to ensure a bountiful harvest, but they also presided over rituals of bloody sacrifice. Their Hindu counterpart, Kali, was the goddess of death; like Coatlicue, her statues were smeared with blood, and she wore a necklace of skulls and a girdle of snakes.

The combined creative and destructive aspects of nature that snakes so often represented were manifested in the annual flooding and receding of Egypt's Nile River. Egyptian goddesses of the earth and sky wore snakes on their foreheads, as did the pharaohs, who became deities at their death. One scholar has written, "All the ideographic theology of Egypt is involved with the cobra." Rather than be taken captive by the Romans, Cleopatra committed suicide by exposing herself to the bite of a cobra (also described as an asp, or horned viper), which was sacred to Isis. Choosing such a death bound her more closely to the great goddess and the hope of immortality.

Before the Hebrews became monotheists, they worshiped snakes. Small bronze serpents, probably cult objects, have been found at several sites in Israel that were sacred to Asherat, the local incarnation of the fertility goddess. There is also a mysterious story in Numbers 21:6–9. While wandering in the desert, the Israelites were attacked by stinging vipers. God commanded Moses to make a ser-

*Helmet mask. Cameroon. Bamileke, Bagam Chiefdom. Nineteenth–twentieth century. Wood with white kaoline pigment, 28″ high. The Metropolitan Museum of Art, New York. Louis V. Bell Fund, 1971*

*Pediment detail of a Gorgon. Corfu. Sixth century BC. Painted limestone. Corfu Museum*

*Cult object. Israelite, Beisan (Beth Shean). Eleventh century BC. Pottery, 19½" high (restored). University of Pennsylvania Museum, Philadelphia*

The exact use of this type of cult object from the United Kingdom is a subject of debate. Perhaps it was used to burn incense; possibly it was used to germinate seeds. If the latter, it can be more closely tied to fertility rituals.

pent out of brass; everyone who looked at it was relieved of pain. Eight hundred years later (according to II Kings 18:4), many Jews worshiped a snake god in the "high places." To return his people to their true faith, Yahweh (Jehovah) told King Hezekiah to "brake in pieces the brasen serpent that Moses had made."

Many Olympian deities—most notably Zeus, Athena, Hermes, and Demeter—had some connection to snakes. In Greece snakes were frequently associated first with goddesses, then with the male gods who gained supremacy over them. Perseus's slaughter of the Gorgon Medusa is often interpreted as a parable of patriarchal victory. Medusa was a daughter of Earth and a sister of the Titans. When her brothers were defeated by Zeus and replaced by the Olympian pantheon, Medusa was banished to "the extreme West," according to Hesiod. The beautiful maiden became a hag. Her features froze in a permanent grimace, and her delicate curls became writhing snakes. Any mortal who looked directly at her turned to stone. To avoid that fate, the hero Perseus sneaked up on Medusa while she slept, watched her reflection in a mirror, and cut off her head.

Medusa's power was passed on to Asclepius, the god of healing, whose shrine at Epidaurus sheltered many snakes. Asclepius learned about medicine from Chiron, the wise centaur who raised him. Athena gave him two vials of Medusa's blood: one killed, the other raised the dead. Asclepius carried a caduceus—a staff with a snake wrapped around it.

The cult of Asclepius spread from Epidaurus to Rome and, throughout the empire, to spas where snakes were already associated with healing. His caduceus—or a variant form with two snakes and wings—was adopted in Roman times as the emblem of physicians, and the connection between snakes and medicine was pervasive. Pliny advocated snake grease as a cure for baldness. According to Germanic myth, Siegfried bathed in dragon's blood to make himself impervious to wounds. The Germans and Celts thought that people could acquire medical knowledge by eating the boiled flesh of a white snake. Many Amerindian tribes ate ritual meals of snake meat, although the Apache and Navajo, in awe of the power attributed to rattlesnakes, had strict taboos against killing or eating them.

The importance of snakes in Amerindian cult practices persists today. The Hopi invoke the help of snakes in their annual dance for rain and a good corn harvest. During the performance, dancers hold newly captured rattlesnakes in their hands and mouths, after which the snakes are released back into the desert. (For decades outsiders wondered how the dancers protected themselves. It has been recently revealed that the snakes are milked or defanged by the priests in whose custody they are placed for several days before the dance.)

The snake-charming fakirs of India also milk their king cobras before performing with them in village marketplaces. This technique was probably practiced for generations by the priests of Kali, Krishna, or other Indian deities. In any case, the fakirs' use of "hypnotic" music is for show. Snakes have no ears and are deaf to airborne sound; the movement of the men and their instruments are what catch the cobras' attention.

In the first years of the twentieth century, George Hensley, a native of Tennessee, founded a new religion based on snake-handling. Hensley was inspired by the biblical text in which Jesus, after the Resurrection, explains the signs of a true believer: "In my name shall they cast out devils, they shall speak with new tongues, they shall take up serpents" (Mark 16:17–18). Hensley's followers put themselves into ecstatic trances and handled snakes to prove that their faith could overcome the devil. Hensley himself was bitten more than four hundred times before a bite on his wrist by a diamondback rattler killed him in 1955.

*Relief of Zeus as a coiled serpent. Cycladic. Fourth century BC. Hymettus marble. Staatliche Museen, Berlin*

*Bertel Thorvaldsen.* Hygeia Feeding the Snake of Asclepius. *1808. Marble, 31⅓″ in diameter. Thorvaldsens Museum, Copenhagen*

Hygeia, sometimes called the goddess of health, was Asclepius's daughter and was often worshiped with him.

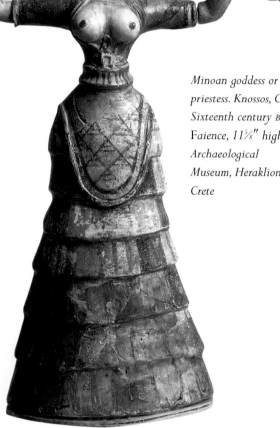

*Minoan goddess or
priestess. Knossos, Crete.
Sixteenth century BC.
Faience, 11⅝" high.
Archaeological
Museum, Heraklion,
Crete*

*Libation vase of Gudea. Sumerian, Lagash. c. 2150 BC. Steatite (soapstone),
8⅞" high. The Louvre, Paris*

Gudea ruled the city of Lagash, which was known in ancient times
as Telloh, for at least fifteen years. He amassed a great body of
public works, including a series of realistic sculptures of himself
between the ages of twenty-five and forty. This libation vase,
inscribed with Gudea's name, is decorated with winged serpents
representing the animal aspects of his patron god and snakes
symbolizing the fertility that enriched his domain.

Akhenaten and Nefertiti *(The Wilbour Plaque). Egyptian. Latter part of the reign of Akhenaten, c. 1352–36 BC. Limestone relief, 6³⁄₁₆ x 8¹¹⁄₁₆ x 1⅛". The Brooklyn Museum, Gift of the Estate of Charles Edwin Wilbour*

*Hagesander, Polydorus, and Athenodorus.* The Laocoön Group. *Rhodian, discovered in 1506 on Esquiline Hill. Probably first century BC or first century AD. Marble. Vatican Museum, Rome*

In Virgil's Aeneid, Laocoön warned his fellow Trojans not to trust the wooden horse and threw his lance at it. In a fury, Athena sent snakes to attack him and his sons, which was interpreted as a sign that Troy was doomed.

Opposite:
*Henry Fuseli.* Thor Battering the Serpent of Midgard. *1790. Oil on canvas, 52 x 36⅔".
Royal Academy of Arts, London*

According to Norse myth, the snake of Midgard—or Earth—was thrown into the sea by Odin; there he wrapped himself around the world and swallowed his tail. His writhing caused storms at sea. After many battles, Thor killed the serpent but was then drowned in the venom that shot out of the dying reptile's mouth.

*Michelangelo da Caravaggio.*
Medusa. *c. 1600. Oil on canvas
on wood, 22″ in diameter. Uffizi
Gallery, Florence*

Several art historians have
speculated that the *Medusa*
is a self-portrait of
Caravaggio.

Opposite:
*Gianlorenzo Bernini.* The Head of
Medusa. *c. 1635. Marble, over lifesize.
Capitoline Museum, Rome*

*Peter Paul Rubens and Frans Snyders.*
The Head of Medusa. *c. 1610–20.*
*Oil on canvas, 27 x 46½".*
*Kunsthistorisches Museum, Vienna*

Art historians believe that Rubens
painted the head of Medusa
while someone else, probably
Snyders, painted the insects and
snakes. The serpents in Medusa's
hair have been identified by a
Harvard herpetologist as common
European grass snakes, but the
coiled snake in the left foreground
has no natural counterpart.
The equally fanciful two-headed
creature in the lower center
corresponds to Pliny's description
of an amphisbaena.

*Parade Shield of Louis XIV. French. c. 1760.*
*Bronze, gold, and silver, 23⅛ x 15¼".*
*The Metropolitan Museum of Art, New York.*
*Rogers Fund, 1904*

Opposite:
*Sir Joshua Reynolds.* Infant Hercules Strangling
the Serpents. *1788. Oil on paper on canvas,*
*23⅞ x 23¾". The John G. Johnson Collection,*
*Philadelphia Museum of Art*

Hercules, or Heracles, was the half-god, half-
mortal son of Zeus and Alcmene. Hera hated
him because he was a proof of Zeus's infideli-
ty. When Heracles was still an infant, Hera
sent two serpents to kill him in the night, but
the baby exhibited his superhuman strength
by strangling the snakes with his bare hands.

*King Njoya of Bamum and his entourage. Cameroon. 1908. Staatliche Museen, Museum für Völkerkunde, Berlin*

Opposite:
*Royal throne and footrest. Bamum, Cameroon. 1908. Wood, covered with colored glass beads, seeds, and cowrie shells, 5' 8" high. Staatliche Museen, Museum für Völkerkunde, Berlin*

The Bamum throne, which was carved from one piece of wood, consists of three main parts—a male figure and a female figure and a stool. The stool is decorated with an interwined double-serpent motif, the most exalted royal symbol for the Bamum people. It may refer to a legendary king from the early nineteenth century who reputedly struck on two military fronts simultaneously to conquer his enemies.

King Njoya inherited the throne from his father. When reports of it reached Germany around the turn of the century, ethnological museums in Berlin, Leipzig, and Stuttgart competed to acquire it. But King Njoya refused to sell or give it away. Finally he agreed to a proposal by the Director of the Museum für Völkerkunde in Berlin to have a copy made, which he planned to give to Emperor Wilhelm II in January 1908 as a birthday gift. As the day drew near, however, the copy was not ready, so the original throne and footrest were sent to Berlin, and King Njoya contented himself with the copy.

*William Blake.* Moses Erecting the Brazen Serpent. *c. 1805. Pen and watercolor over pencil, 13⅜ x 12¾".*
*Courtesy, Museum of Fine Arts, Boston. Purchased 1890*

Buddha Meditating on the Naga
Mucalinda. *Cambodian, in the style
of Angkor Wat. Late eleventh—twelfth
century. Sandstone, 3′6″ high. Musée
Guimet, Paris*

Lord Krishna Dancing with Seven-Headed Cobra.
*Indian. Sixteenth century. Bronze, 25½″ high.
By Courtesy of the Board of Trustees of the Victoria &
Albert Museum, London*

Page 48:
*Plumed Serpent (Quetzalcoatl).
Aztec. Fifteenth century. Stone, 20¹⁄₁₆″
high. Pontificio Museo Missionario-
Etnologico, The Vatican, Rome*

Page 49:
*Goddess (Coatlicue). Aztec. Twelfth—
fifteenth century* AD. *Stone,
approximately 8′6″ high. National
Museum of Anthropology, Mexico City*

# THE TEMPTER
## IN THE GARDEN

*François Fouquet. "Le Péché Originel" (detail). From* Manuscrit de la Cité de Dieu. *c. 1473. Bibliothèque Nationale, Paris*

Soon after God created Eve from Adam's rib, Eve was confronted by a snake. The snake tempted her to taste the fruit of the tree standing in the middle of Eden, "for God doth know that in the day ye eat thereof, then your eyes shall be opened; and ye shall be as gods, knowing good and evil" (Genesis 3:5).

The early rabbis wondered how the serpent spoke with Eve. They concluded that, while other animals could talk with each other in animal language, only the snake knew Hebrew. In punishment after the Fall, the serpent's tongue was split and all it could do was hiss. The rabbis taught that many animals were changed after the Creation—the mole lost its eye, the frog lost its teeth—but the snake's transformation was the most drastic of all. Before tempting Eve, the serpent had stood upright on two legs like a man and was as tall as a camel. Afterward, God hacked off its hands and feet and forced it to eat dirt. Its superior intelligence, however, remained.

The Fall brought sin and death into the world. For centuries, religious teachers, storytellers, and artists—all of them male—examined every detail of the transgression. They exonerated Adam and blamed Eve and the snake for all the subsequent suffering of the human race.

Monotheists wanted to distance themselves from the pagan cult practices in which goddesses and snakes had been worshiped for millennia. According to the patriarchal religions, demonic sexuality was the essence of Eve's female nature, in contrast to the purity, asceticism, and rationality that characterized the best of masculinity. Church fathers valued celibacy, or at least marriage; they believed that men could conquer their lust, whereas women were dominated by their sexual desires. The phallic snake offered Eve what she wanted most.

Some Christian commentators on Genesis believed the serpent desired Eve. Others said that, in eating the apple, Eve symbolically had intercourse with the snake, which awakened her desire and encouraged her to seduce Adam.

Learned opinion was divided: Did the snake act on his own or was he the agent of the devil? By the Middle Ages, it was widely believed that the serpent was Satan himself. Accordingly, the representation by artists of the events in the garden began to change.

Opposite:
*Hans Baldung Grien.* Eve, the Serpent, and Death. *c. 1510–12. Oil on wood, 25 x 12⅔". National Gallery of Canada, Ottawa*

Grien was the first artist to create a large-scale work in which Death is a major character in the Temptation. He thereby acknowledged the most important consequence of Eve's disobedience—the fact that she and her descendants must die. By having the serpent bind Death to the tree, Grien explicated the Christian doctrine that knowledge is sinful and humanity's desire for it leads to death.

Before the twelfth century, scenes of the Temptation showed three figures: a snake wrapped around the tree, Adam, and Eve. As the devil emerged as a more active player, the drama shifted to the tension between the snake and Eve.

By the twelfth century, the snake had begun to acquire a human, usually female, face. A churchman, Peter Comestor, supported this interpretation in his writing. In the ancient world, monsters like sphinxes, sirens, and harpies had female faces, so it was logical, Comestor reasoned, that the snake had one, too. If womenkind were inherently wicked, the argument went on, the snake could be an aspect or a reflection of Eve herself. Comestor's implied misogyny was common among medieval scholars, who believed that Eve was vulnerable to temptation because she was morally weaker than Adam; or because she was vain and susceptible to flattery; or because she was greedy; or because she was less rational than her spouse.

The convention of a snake with a human face spread to the theater and to popular literature. In late fourteenth-century miracle plays, the actor playing the serpent of the Temptation was often costumed as a sphinx. In *Piers Plowman,* the devil appears as a lizard with a female face.

Many Renaissance artists in Catholic Italy, among them Masolino, Raphael, and Michelangelo, painted the snake as a fair-haired beauty who looked very much like Eve. Protestants, on the other hand, believed that there was no basis in Scripture for anthropomorphizing the serpent, and Lutheran-influenced masters like Albrecht Dürer and Lucas Cranach depicted their snakes as snakes.

With the Enlightenment and increasing secularization, commentators and artists treated the story of Adam and Eve less as a tale of original sin and more as a humanistic parable. The tension between religious determinism and free will dominated philosophical discourse for the next two hundred years. The temptation in Eden retained its centrality in Western mythology, but it was stripped of dogma. Eating the apple became a more positive act—a metaphor for human individuation, rejection of innocence, and the acquisition of knowledge for its own sake. The snake thus became an aid to Adam and Eve's education rather than an accomplice to their crime. But while the first couple may have been admired for their intellectual quest, the snake never received credit for being their guide.

*Erastus Salisbury Field.*
*The Garden of Eden. c. 1865.*
*Oil on canvas, 35 x 41½".*
*The Shelburne Museum, Vermont*

*Masolino.* Adam and Eve: The Fall. *c. 1425.*
*Fresco, 83½ x 34⅔". Brancacci Chapel, Santa Maria*
*del Carmine, Florence*

Opposite:
*Lucas Cranach the Elder.* Eve. *First half of the sixteenth*
*century. Oil on wood, 33½ x 25⅓". Koninklijk Museum*
*voor Schone Kunsten, Antwerp*

Eve and a Female-Headed Serpent by the Tree of Paradise. *Flemish. Fifteenth century. Boxwood base for a statuette, 3½ x 4¹³⁄₁₆". The Metropolitan Museum of Art, New York. The Cloisters Collection*

Opposite:
*Hugo van der Goes. The Temptation. c. 1470–80. Oil on oak panel, 15¼ x 9". Kunsthistorisches Museum, Vienna*

Van der Goes's Edenic snake is a unique creation: a lizard-like reptile with a woman's head and horns formed from plaits of hair.

*Max Klinger. "The Snake."*
*Plate 3 from the cycle*
Eve and the Future.
*c. 1880. Etching, 16¼ x*
*11⅝". Private collection,*
*courtesy Galerie St. Etienne,*
*New York*

*Paul Gauguin.* Eve. *1889. Watercolor and pastel on paper, 13¼ x 12¼". Bequest of Marion Koogler McNay, McNay Art Museum, San Antonio, Texas*

The French painter Gauguin was always searching for a way back to Paradise. In ceramics and in paintings, he turned often to the subject of Eve and the problem of temptation. Here Eve covers her ears to avoid hearing the serpent's seductive hiss.

*Michelangelo Buonarroti.* The Fall. *1508–12. Fresco. The Sistine Chapel, The Vatican, Rome*

The Fall left mankind, in John Milton's words, "to Sin and Death a prey." For Christians, belief in Jesus Christ and the sacraments of the church offered the only deliverance from their inherited destiny. The church fathers scoured the Old Testament for prophetic evidence to substantiate their faith.

In the story of the Edenic serpent's fate, they found a foretelling of Redemption. God's promise that Eve's seed would bruise the snake's head was interpreted as a prophecy that the Son of God would crush evil in the form of the satanic serpent. Christian folklore and art ascribed this triumph to the baby Jesus, although no such story appears in the Gospels. Perhaps it echoes the legend of the infant Hercules, who subdued serpents in his cradle.

In some paintings of Jesus' death on Golgotha, a serpent at the feet of the crucified Christ indicates His victory over evil and death. The Old Testament story of the brazen serpent, which Moses erected at God's command, was taken as a prefiguration of Christ dying on the Cross for mankind's sins. According to John 3:14–15, "And as Moses lifted up the serpent in the wilderness, even so must the Son of man be lifted up: That whosoever believeth in him should not perish, but have eternal life."

The English Romantic poet and artist William Blake (1757–1827), obsessed with the struggle between good and evil, was, not surprisingly, also obsessed with snakes. They probably appear more frequently in his paintings, drawings, and engravings than in the work of any other artist. Blake's idiosyncratic religion encompassed a good God, who created spirit, and a bad god, whom he called Urizen, who created matter. Blake equated materialism with the worship of the evil god.

In Blake's writings as well as his art, snakes represent various forms of evil. A snake may stand for hypocrisy, restrictions on individual freedom, or the power of the clergy. Sometimes serpents stand for carnal pleasure. Blake believed that sexuality was good if it was part of the sacrament of true love but bad when it was an expression of lust or the impulse to dominate.

Judas. *Mexican. Acajete, Puebla. c. 1960. Painted plaster, 23″ high. The Girard Foundation Collection, Museum of International Folk Art, A Unit of the Museum of New Mexico, Santa Fe*

*William Blake.* Satan, Sin and Death, *from* Paradise Lost. *1808. Pen and watercolor, 19½ x 15¹³⁄₁₆″. The Henry E. Huntington Library and Art Gallery, San Marino, California*

Opposite:
*William Blake.* The Descent of Typhon and the Gods into Hell (The Old Dragon): Milton's Hymn on the Morning of Christ's Nativity, *from* Paradise Lost. *The Thomas Set, 1809. Pen and watercolor, 9⅞ x 7½″. The Whitworth Art Gallery, Manchester, England*

Blake had a lifelong fascination with the works of John Milton (1608–1674). He wrote a long illustrated poem about Milton and made several sets of illustrations for Milton's *Paradise Lost,* but he modified Milton's puritanical interpretation of the Bible. Blake believed that Milton was too reticent about human sexuality. And his illustrations often portray the snake with some sympathy, as if to acknowledge that the evil impulse is an inherent component of human nature.

*Agnolo Bronzino, The Brazen Serpent, c. 1540–64. Fresco. Palazzo Vecchio, Chapel of Eleonora of Toledo, Florence*

*William Blake.* Michael Foretelling the Crucifixion to Adam, *from* Paradise Lost. *1808. Pen and watercolor, 19¾ x 15″. Courtesy, Museum of Fine Arts, Boston. Gift by Subscription*

Blake believed that the corporeal Jesus had human lusts and desires. For Blake, the serpent at the base of the cross, in addition to linking Christ to the Old Testament prophecy, also acknowledges that he was a sexual being like the rest of humankind.

Opposite:
*Jan Vermeer.* Allegory of the Faith. *c. 1672. Oil on canvas, 45 x 35″. The Metropolitan Museum of Art, New York. Bequest of Michael Friedsam, 1931. The Friedsam Collection*

# DRAGONS AND
# OTHER FANCIFUL CREATURES

I n his *Natural History,* Pliny reported that snakes in India grew so large they could swallow stags and bulls whole. "These stories are credible," he wrote, "because of the serpents in Italy called boas, which reach such dimensions that during the principate of Claudius of blessed memory a whole child was found in the belly of one that was killed on the Vatican Hill."

Pliny also described a creature called a basilisk. Said to be a native of Cyrenaica, the basilisk was nearly a foot long, with a reptilian body and a bright, white, crownlike marking on its head. It had an idiosyncratic way of moving; unlike ordinary snakes, it did not slither but moved straight ahead, "with its middle raised high." Its poison was so deadly that a man on horseback once killed a basilisk "and the infection rising through the spear killed not only the rider but also the horse."

In the second century AD, a writer named Physiologus, thought to be a Christian ascetic living in Alexandria, wrote a natural history that combined folklore and science from writers like Pliny, Aristotle, and Herodotus with stories from the Bible. Physiologus collected stories about fifty-some animals in an attempt to deduce religious truths from them. His work became the prototype for books called bestiaries—allegorical and moralizing accounts of real animals and imaginary ones that were widely believed to exist. Illustrated bestiaries were popular in the twelfth and thirteenth centuries, especially in England; the texts provided teaching tools for clerics, and the pictures delighted a wider lay public. Bestiary animals were copied in other illuminated manuscripts, carved on churches, and painted on shields and banners. They were also alluded to in poetry and romance literature.

According to bestiaries, fabulous beasts like unicorns, harpies, and monkfish (half-monk, half-fish) coexisted in the natural world with lions, boars, and elephants. Compilers of the books acknowledged having difficulty in classifying some animals, among them snakes. Included in the category of *serpentes* were snakelike creatures with legs and even wings but not fur or feathers.

Pliny's old nemesis the basilisk—half-cock, half-reptile—reappeared as an image of the devil. Bestiaries also included such snakelike creatures as the amphisbaena, which had

*"St. Margaret and the Dragon."*
*From the* Hours of the Virgin,
*M. 19, folio 157v. French or*
*Flemish. 1430–40. The Pierpont*
*Morgan Library, New York*

*Bishop's crosier (St. Michael and the Dragon).*
*French, Limoges. Late twelfth–early thirteenth*
*century. Champlevé enamel on copper-gilt.*
*The Metropolitan Museum of Art, New York.*
*Bequest of Michael Friedsam, 1931.*
*The Friedsam Collection*

two venomous heads; the hydrus, a benign Nile serpent; the boa, which sucked from cows' udders; the jaiculus, often winged, which attacked its prey from trees; and seps and dipsa, two snakes so poisonous that the bodies of their victims disintegrated instantly. Some of these creatures were obviously based on cobras, constrictors, and vipers, but the relatively high number of snakes in these cautionary tales was the authors' way of dramatizing the pervasiveness of evil in the world.

The most common medieval monster was the dragon. (*Draco,* the Latin word, can be translated variously as "dragon," "serpent," or "snake," as can the Greek, *drakon.*) In bestiaries the dragon was usually depicted as a kind of gigantic non-poisonous serpent that could crush its victim, even one as large as an elephant. Dragons were evoked to remind people of the power of Satan, who ambushed God-fearing people, tempted them away from the path toward heaven, ensnared them in his tenacious coils, and dragged them to hell.

The dragon in its more familiar guise as a scaly, bat-winged, fire-breathing monster was the most compelling medieval symbol of sin. Its gaping jaws were the gates of hell; the flames issuing from its mouth were the fires that roasted the damned. The Catholic church canonized any champion who could vanquish such a demonic creature. Michael, George, and Margaret of Antioch are the most famous Christian saints remembered for their triumphs over dragons.

The twelfth chapter of Revelations records a "war in heaven," in which "a great red dragon, having seven heads and ten horns, and seven crowns upon his heads . . . stood before [a] woman which was ready to be delivered, for to devour her child as soon as it was born." The archangel Michael, the protector of Israel, challenged the dragon and prevailed against him, "and the great dragon was cast out, that old serpent, called the Devil, and Satan, which deceiveth the whole world."

Like Michael, George slew a dragon to protect a vulnerable woman. The exploits of Michael and George recall the Greek legend of Perseus rescuing Andromeda from the rock at Jaffa, where she awaited her sacrifice to a sea monster. The dragon was preeminent among those ancient mythical beasts who could be invested with satanic intent in the service of Christian teaching.

There are many local variants to the story of Saint George. In a typical account, George, a Roman tribune born in Cappadocia, encountered a terrible

*"Crocodile and Serpent." From the Roy 12 C. XIX Manuscript, folio 12v. English. Late twelfth century. British Library, London*

The crocodile and the serpent (or the hydrus, in some accounts) were natural enemies. The hydrus coated itself with mud and slid into the gaping mouth of a crocodile asleep on the banks of the Nile. Startled, the crocodile swallowed the hydrus whole. The hydrus then burst out of the evil creature's belly, through its skin, killing it and emerging unharmed. The story was an allegory of Christ in earthly form, descending into Hell to free people condemned there unfairly.

dragon whose poisonous breath threatened the inhabitants of a Libyan city. The townspeople placated the beast with sacrifices of sheep and children, but the dragon was not satisfied. Finally the king was forced to offer his daughter, Saba. George, passing by, heard her crying and swore to destroy the dragon in Christ's name. He killed the monster, had everyone in the city baptized, and went on to become one of Christianity's most popular saints. His deeds are memorialized in stained-glass windows, medieval manuscripts, and paintings by masters of the High Renaissance. George was already honored as the patron saint of England when Edward III installed him as protector of the Knights of the Garter during the Hundred Years' War.

Margaret of Antioch is described as a virgin who rejected the devil's advances at least three times before he took the form of a dragon and swallowed her. In his belly, Margaret made the sign of the cross, the monster burst apart (or, in other

Amphisbaena. *Detail of archway from St. Cosmus, Narbonne. French (Languedoc). Second half of the twelfth century. The Metropolitan Museum of Art, New York. Kennedy Fund, 1922. The Cloisters Collection*

The amphisbaena had two heads, one at each end of its body, both poisonous. When one head was awake, the other slept. Sometimes one head would grasp the other in its jaws so that the animal could roll like a hoop. Because the amphisbaena could presumably move in either direction, it was a symbol of wayward and ungodly behavior.

versions, vomited her up), and the pious maiden was saved. Once again good triumphed over evil, Christianity over paganism.

Perhaps nowhere have dragons been more popular than in China, where they have always been auspicious. Much like the snake deities and icons of early Middle Eastern and Indian cultures, the Chinese dragon was associated with rain, fecundity, power, and good fortune. (Some scholars believe the creature was first invented and revered in Mesopotamia from whence its devotees carried it to China; others believe the reverse.) As the Chinese spirit of water, mist, and rain, the dragon ruled the great Yangtze and Yellow rivers, the sky, and the sea.

Stylized dragons are the most common ornamental motif in early Chinese art; they appear on bronzes and jades of the Shang and Zhou dynasties (eighteenth–third centuries BC). Dragons appear on sacred robes, ivory carvings, lacquered vessels, and blue-and-white porcelains from the Ming and Qing eras (late fourteenth–early twentieth centuries AD). Sumptuary laws from the time of the thirteenth-century Mongol ruler Kublai Khan reserved for the emperor the right to have five-clawed dragons embroidered on his robes; aristocrats and other high-ranking officials were restricted to four-clawed beasts. In Japan (and at times in China as well), a three-clawed dragon denoted imperial status.

The dragon remains a potent symbol in Asia. The Year of the Dragon is a time of good luck, and everyone born during its passage is presumed to be blessed.

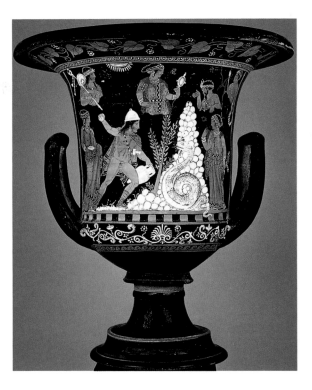

*Attributed to the Python Painter.* Kadmos Fighting the Dragon. *Greek, Paestum. c. 340 BC. Krater, 22¼″ high. The Louvre, Paris*

Above left:
Thetis and the Serpent. *English, by Wedgwood. 1871. Majolica platter, 15″ in diameter. Courtesy Nicholas Dawes*

*Compact. French, by Cartier; Chinoiserie signed by Vladimir Makovsky. 1927. Gold with red and black enamel, rose-cut diamonds, European Chinoiserie of a mother-of-pearl dragon and waves. Courtesy Cartier Collection, Geneva*

Europeans were fascinated by Chinoiserie, and to a lesser extent, Japonaiserie, after the mid-nineteenth century when Asia opened its doors to Western traders. Cartier produced many pieces featuring the motif of the Chinese dragon.

Above:
*"Adder and Mate." From the Harley 4751 Manuscript, folio 60r. English. c. 1230–40. British Library, London*

The adder was a creature with insatiable sexual appetites and a tumultuous life cycle. In the act of passion, the male adder stuck his head inside the mouth of his mate, who promptly bit it off. Her fate was equally violent: her unborn young were so impatient to emerge that they gnawed a hole in her abdomen to get out. The unhappy story of the adder was a plea for marital harmony.

*"Basilisk." From the Harley 4751 Manuscript, folio 59. English. c. 1230–40. British Library, London*

The basilisk was king of the serpents, an allegorical representation of the devil. Basilisks had red eyes that could kill with a glance and therefore had to be approached with mirrors, like Medusa. Basilisks could also kill by biting or hissing, and sometimes even their odor was deadly.

spif uocata qd morfu uenena infitit & fpar
git. Iof, eñ greci uenenu dicunt. & inde afpif
q morfu uenenato infitit. Ofrut qd dr fep pa

*"Asp Stopping Ear." From the Harley 4751 Manuscript, folio 61r. English. c. 1230–40. British Library, London*

The asp, or adder (the names are interchangeable), could be enticed from its lair by the music of an enchanter, so the creature tried to shut out the sound by pushing one ear against the ground and closing the other with its long tail. For the writers of bestiaries, the asp represented greedy men who seek earthly rewards but turn a deaf ear to God: "They are like the deaf adder that stoppeth her ear; which will not hearken to the voice of the charmers, charming never so wisely" (Psalm 58:4–5).

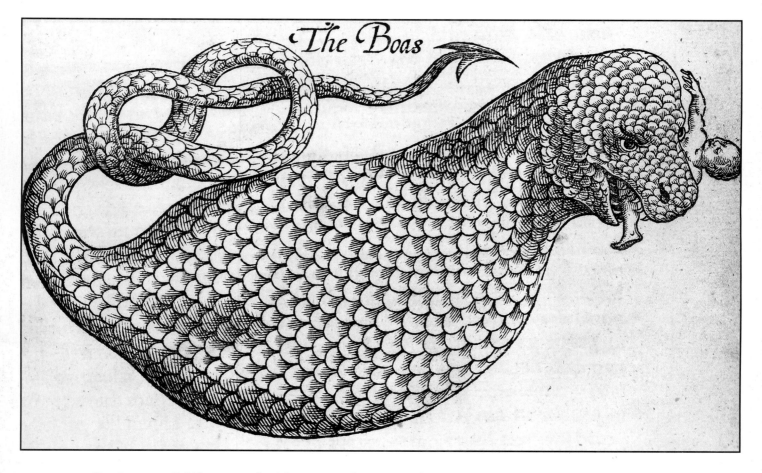

The Boas

*"Boa Devouring Child." Engraving from* The History of Four-Footed Beasts, Serpents, and Insects, *by Edward Topsell. London, 1658. Rare Books and Manuscript Division, The New York Public Library, Astor, Lenox and Tilden Foundations*

Opposite:
*Engraving from* An Essay Towards a Natural History of Serpents, *by Charles Owen. London, 1742. General Research Division, The New York Public Library, Astor, Lenox and Tilden Foundations*

*The Common Asp*

*The Winged Dragon*

*The Ethiopian Dragon*

*The Scytale*

*Imperial court robe, back. Chinese. Qing dynasty, c. 1644–61. Silk and metal tapestry, 56″ long. The Metropolitan Museum of Art, New York. Bequest of William Christian Paul, 1929*

*Dragon plaque. Chinese. Warring states period, fifth–fourth century BC. Hammered gold foil, 4¹¹⁄₁₆″ long. Courtesy Weisbrod Chinese Art, Ltd., New York*

The creature in the plaque has the back-turned head of a dragon at one end and the head of a bird with a curving beak at the other.

Pages 82–83:

*Roof ornament. Chinese. Ming dynasty, sixteenth century. Enamel glaze on ceramic, 17⅞ x 31⅝″. Courtesy Weisbrod Chinese Art, Ltd., New York*

Because of their association with rain, dragons such as this were frequently placed at the corner of a roof to ward off lightning.

*Attributed to Ignaz Preissler*. Attilius Regulus Battling the African Serpent. *c. 1720–25. Chinese porcelain with painting, 11″ in diameter. The Nelson-Atkins Museum of Art, Kansas City, acquired through the generosity of Mr. and Mrs. Earl D. Wilberg, 1985*

The Roman consul Attilius Regulus battles a giant serpent, representing Carthage, Rome's enemy. Regulus had many victories over the Carthaginians, though he was defeated by them once, in 255 BC. The connection between Carthage and the serpent probably comes from a story told by Pliny about Regulus killing a 120-foot-long python during his African campaigns. The Latin inscription on the reverse of the dish states, "Roman Consul Attilius Regulus, at last a victor, has overcome by means of the bow, the dart, the spear, and the javelin, with much slaughter of his own men, the African serpent, menacing because of its vibrating tongue and terrifying because of its circular movement."

Opposite:
*Aquamanile (Dragon Swallowing a Man). German. Late twelfth–early thirteenth century. Bronze, 8¾″ high. The Metropolitan Museum of Art, New York. The Cloisters Collection, 1947*

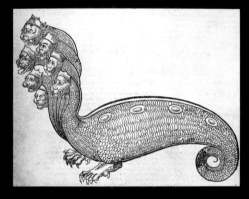

*"Hydra." Engraving from* The History of
Four-Footed Beasts, Serpents, and Insects,
*by Edward Topsell. London, 1658. Rare Books
and Manuscript Division, The New York Public
Library, Astor, Lenox and Tilden Foundations*

Opposite:
*Gustave Moreau.* Hercules and the
Lernaean Hydra. *1876. Oil on canvas,
61 x 52". The Art Institute of Chicago.
Gift of Mrs. Eugene A. Davidson*

# THE SNAKE OBSERVED

A lbertus Seba (1665–1736), a prosperous Amsterdam apothecary with a passion for natural history, traveled to the East and West Indies at the start of the eighteenth century, collecting mammals, birds, reptiles, scorpions, shells, echinoderms, and other specimens from the animal, vegetable, and mineral kingdoms. He gave medicine to sailors in exchange for exotica they had brought back from distant ports.

Seba sold his collection—the most remarkable of its day—to Peter the Great in 1717 and promptly amassed a new one. His second "cabinet of curiosities" soon outgrew the first. He kept his treasures in hermetically sealed jars, attempting to preserve as much of their original coloration and shape as possible.

Seba's wonders were painted and engraved by many of his contemporaries. Copperplate engravings by Pieter Tanje of an eclectic variety of creatures are prominent in Seba's four-volume opus entitled *Locupletissimi Rerum Naturalium Thesauri (The Most Abundant Treasures of Nature),* published between 1734 and 1765. The engravings in Seba's work provided the most vivid and accurate representation of the world's snakes available at the time.

Seba assembled and displayed his objects to inform the public about the wonders of the natural world. His enterprise typified the humanistic spirit of his age. Its antecedents included the great library at Alexandria, founded by Ptolemy in the third century BC, and the private collections of rulers like Solomon or Alexander. During the Middle Ages, the great monasteries accumulated exotic artifacts donated by travelers returning from pilgrimages to the Holy Land or other exotic places.

In the sixteenth and seventeenth centuries, naturalists began to study rocks, minerals, flowers, and plants. Private collections of natural objects—like those of the Swiss naturalist Conrad Gesner and of Bernard Palissy (1510–1590), a well-known Huguenot potter—were as common as collections of art. The joy that people found in learning about rare specimens and novel creatures from faraway lands allowed for a certain naive confusion of the odd with the impossible. Many of these collections placed so-called unicorn horns and giants' bones authoritatively next to mummies, human skulls, and fossil shells. Seba endorsed more rigorous standards. He displayed the famous seven-

*J. Sera.* Crotalus durissus. *Hand-colored lithograph, from* North American Herpetology or, A Description of the Reptiles Inhabiting the United States, *vol. 3, plate 1, by John Edwards Holbrook, Philadelphia, 1842. The New York Public Library, Astor, Lenox and Tilden Foundations*

Holbrook's Latin nomenclature is considered obsolete, but not incorrect, by twentieth-century herpetologists. According to Holbrook, *C. durissus* (now identified as the canebrake rattler, *Crotalus horridus atri caudatus*) has the greatest range of any rattlesnake in the United States; it is found nearly everywhere in the country. He dismisses the commonly held belief (stated firmly by Seba, among others) that the number of rattles marks the age of the animal, much like the rings of a tree. Holbrook recognizes that rattlers can gain or lose rattles depending on their health or food supply.

headed "Hamburg" hydra in his reptile exhibit with the explanation that the monster had been stitched together from parts of various animals.

As early as 1559, Gesner had conceived a classification of animals by genera and species. His *Historia Animalium* marked the beginning of modern zoology, just as Carolus Linnaeus's *Systema Naturae* (1735) set forth the foundations of modern taxonomic nomenclature. Informed by this scientific vision, motivated by curiosity, and avid for wealth or fame, collectors and scholars competed with each other for new discoveries. The Fellows of the Royal Society of London for Improving Natural Knowledge sponsored adventurers who traveled throughout the expanding British empire and other foreign lands to send specimens back to London.

As the North American continent was colonized from the Atlantic to the Rockies, explorers came across peoples, animals, and plants that no European had ever seen before. They often recorded what they saw in journals and in paintings so that Europeans and, later, the settled colonists on the East Coast could share their excitement. To disseminate these images more widely, their works were reproduced as prints, engraved and bound in books.

Mark Catesby (1682/3–1749) spent ten years in the colonies, first as a traveler and collector, then as a commissioned scientific recorder and painter. In 1712, he arrived in Williamsburg to explore the surrounding region and to gather specimens and seeds, which he shipped back to England. He returned with sponsorship in 1722 and spent four years collecting and painting along the Eastern seaboard and in the Bahamas. He ran into trouble when sailors opened jars of his animal specimens and drank the rum in which they were preserved for the voyage home.

While working in South Carolina, Catesby came up against many rattlesnakes, one of which was eighteen feet long. In a letter to a friend during the winter of 1722–23, he recounted a close call:

> A Negro woman making my bed, a few minutes after I was out of it, cryed out a Rattle Snake. We being drinking Tea in the next room, which was a ground flore, and being surprised with the vehemence of the wenches bauling, went to see the cause, and found, as the wench had said, a Rattle Snake actually between the sheets in the very place I lay, vigorous and full of ire, biting at everything that approach'd him. Probably It crept in for warmth

in the Night; but how long I had the company of [the] charming Bedfellow I am not able to say.

Catesby tried to dispel folklore and myths about snakes. His sponsors insisted he send back plants reputed to cure snakebites, but he understood that the severity of a bite depended more on the location of the wound and the species of snake than on any remedy. "Where a vein or Artery is pricked by the bite of a Rattle Snake," he wrote, "no Antidote will avail anything, but Death certainly and Suddainly ensues, sometimes in two or three minutes, which I have more than once seen." He also observed that the Indians "know their destiny the minute they are bit; and when they perceive it mortal, apply no other remedy, concluding all efforts [to be] in vain."

Catesby attacked other herpetological apocrypha. He said he had never seen anything to support the belief, common to Linnaeus and others, that the North American rattlesnake bewitched birds and squirrels with its eyes so that they fell from the limb of a tree into its open mouth. He also denied that the tail of a water moccasin was as deadly as its head or that a "coach-whip snake" could rip a man in half by the lash of its tail.

In the 1730s, Catesby made etchings of his watercolors of plants and wildlife, which were eventually published in *The Natural History of Carolina, Florida, and the Bahama Islands*—the first general work on American flora and fauna published in English. He also wrote the text and, in the first edition, hand-colored most of the prints. In the book's preface, he wrote, "As I was not bred a Painter, I hope some faults in Perspective, and other niceties, may be more readily excused." Catesby's modesty was unwarranted; his work was unmatched for nearly a century.

John James Audubon (1785–1851), born in what is now Haiti, was the illegitimate son of a French lieutenant and his mistress. Raised in France on a farm in the Loire Valley, where he spent hours hunting and drawing wild birds, Audubon migrated to America in 1803 to manage his father's Pennsylvania farm. He studied birds in the wild and learned to wire newly killed specimens so that they retained their natural postures for his sketches.

Noted bird painter Alexander Wilson, the editor of *American Ornithology*, convinced Audubon that his work was worthy of publication. At the age of thirty-five,

Audubon began a project to document all the birds of America in their natural habitats. Six years later, in 1826, he sailed to England to find a publisher. Against all advice, he insisted that his work be reproduced as hand-colored life-size aquatints, printed in double elephant folios, from copperplates two feet wide and three feet long. After more than a decade, the complete *Birds of America* was published to his specifications, in four volumes, which sold for $1,000 the set.

Audubon liked to reproduce dramatic scenes when he came upon them. While sketching a nest of brown thrashers in an oak tree, he saw a black snake nearly crush a female bird who was defending her eggs. Two males tried to frighten the snake away. At the time, Audubon's critics challenged the scene, saying that snakes could not climb trees, but Audubon has since been vindicated in his observation. Similarly, his controversial depiction of a viper's fangs turned inward has also been substantiated.

The life and work of John Edwards Holbrook, M.D. (1794–1871), perhaps the most comprehensive chronicler of American snakes, culminated in the 1842 publication of his magisterial five-volume work on North American herpetology. Holbrook's books included accurately colored drawings of venomous and nonvenomous species with detailed observations of their habits. The rattlesnake, for example, which lives on rabbits and squirrels, is a "remarkably slow and sluggish animal, lying quietly in wait for his prey, and never wantonly attacking nor destroying animals, except as food, unless disturbed by them. A single touch, however, will effect this; even rustling the leaves in his neighborhood is sufficient to irritate him."

Holbrook debunked the story told by Catesby about the rattler in his bed, maintaining that Catesby's servants had deceived him because rattlesnakes are never "abroad" in cold weather. Holbrook, like other naturalists before and since, took pains to point out the timidity of most snakes: "In his native woods one may pass within a few feet of [a rattlesnake] unmolested; though aware of the passenger's presence, he either lies quiet or glides away to a more retired spot." While acknowledging that venomous snakes were "regarded with universal abhorrence," Holbrook knew that they posed less of a threat to people than the reverse.

*Antoine-Louis Barye.* Python Killing a Gnu. *1834–35. Bronze, 8⅓″ high. Walters Art Gallery, Baltimore*

Barye, a close observer of animal anatomy and behavior, made several studies of a live python with prey, incorporating in various works the way it encircled, suffocated, and then swallowed its kill.

*Bernard Palissy. Plate. c. 1565. Lead-glazed molded earthenware, 10½″ in diameter.*
*By Courtesy of the Board of Trustees of the Victoria & Albert Museum, London*

Palissy's works are notable for their unusual colors and sea-life motifs.
His pottery was widely imitated, even in his day, and is mostly unsigned,
so attributions are difficult. Palissy's naturalistic treatment of sea creatures,
worms, and insects makes many people squeamish.

Opposite:
*Otto Marseus van Schrieck.* Joseph's Coat Surrounded by a Snake, a Lizard, and Butterflies.
*1669. Oil on panel, 23⅖ x 18¾″. Private collection*

Otto Marseus van Schrieck was famous as the initiator of "herb pieces"—still lifes depicting plants
and animals in an ostensibly natural environment, often near a tree trunk or cave. Although the
individual subjects are accurately depicted, they are seldom encountered together in nature or
in such profusion. In this painting, the most prominent plants include a leafless cyclamen
(*C. hederifolium*) blooming on the left and a Joseph's Coat (*Amaranthus tricolor*) in the foreground;
seven species of butterflies and a dragonfly can also be identified. A poisonous adder (*Vivera aspis*),
native to Italy, is poised to attack a sand lizard (*Lacerta agilis*).

 Snakes do not usually chase lizards, nor do lizards hunt butterflies. The works of Van Schrieck
and his followers, which seem to be nature studies, are in fact morality plays. They are meant to
reflect a pessimistic view of the world, and the snake, once again, symbolizes evil and death.

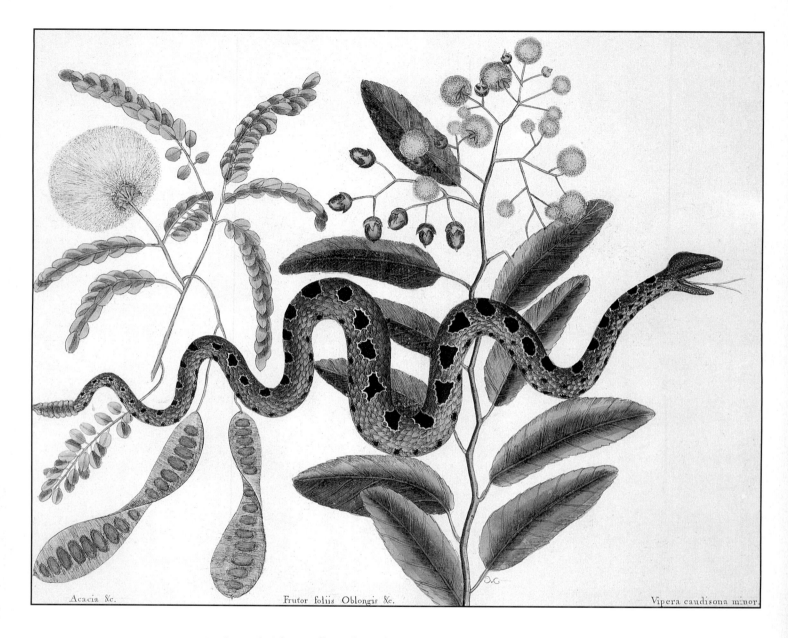

Acacia &c.    Frutor foliis Oblongis &c.    Vipera caudisona minor.

*Mark Catesby.* The Small Rattle-Snake. *Hand-colored etching, from* The Natural History of Carolina, Florida, and the Bahama Islands, *vol. 2, plate 42. London, 1743. Courtesy W. Graham Arader III, New York*

Opposite:
*Mark Catesby.* The Green Spotted Snake. *Hand-colored etching, from* The Natural History of Carolina, Florida, and the Bahama Islands, *vol. 2, plate 53. London, 1743. Courtesy W. Graham Arader III, New York*

In general, Catesby's identification was accurate, although his nomenclature has been superseded. This snake is now called the Carolina Pygmy rattler. The green snake on the opposite page is probably the Eastern garter snake.

Apocynum &c.

Anguis &c.

*Maria Sibylla Merian. "Crocodile of Surinam." 1717. Hand-colored etching, from* Dissertation sur la generation et les transformations des insectes de Surinam, *by Maria Sibylla Merian*

Merian was a remarkable German artist and scientist, who, after being ignored for years, has recently been accorded her rightful place among the pioneers of modern zoology. With her daughter, Merian traveled to South America in 1699; it was probably the first trip to the New World taken by a European for the purpose of scientific fieldwork.

This crocodile is more properly a cayman, and the snake can be identified as *Anilius scytale*, which is common in Surinam. It does not eat snails, although many

Aspis, Aegyptiaca, permagna *(no. 1),* Aspis, Ceilonica, rubra *(no. 2). 1734–35. Hand-colored engraving, from* Locupletissimi Rerum Naturalium Thesauri, *by Albertus Seba. Courtesy O'Shea Gallery, London*

Seba asserts that the large red snake was worshiped by the Egyptians.

N.º 3.

N.º 6.

N.º 2.

N.º 1.

Vipera, Orientalis, maxima Caudisona, femina *(no. 1)*, Serpens, Bojobi, Brasiliensis *(no. 2). 1734–35. Hand-colored engraving, from* Locupletissimi Rerum Naturalium Thesauri, *by Albertus Seba. Courtesy O'Shea Gallery, London*

Of the *Vipera orientalis,* Seba writes that inhabitants of Guatemala call it Teuthlacoth zanphui—the ruler of snakes—because of its notorious wickedness and the frightening sound it makes as it creeps along. Further, it has forty rattles; therefore, it is forty years old, since each year it gets a new rattle. The blue snake, according to Seba, sometimes lives in houses. Though normally benign, it can be dangerous if aroused because of the way it tears flesh with its teeth.

Serpens, Brasiliensis *(no. 1)*, Serpentes, Americana *(nos. 2, 3)*, Serpens, Americana, Lemniscata *(no. 4)*. *1734–35. Hand-colored engraving, from* Locupletissimi Rerum Naturalium Thesauri, *by Albertus Seba. Courtesy O'Shea Gallery, London*

Of the two intertwined snakes at bottom, Seba writes that they fight over territory: "They don't bite, but they batter each other with so much force that they seem to tear each other apart. They separate only when they are exhausted. Some people might say that what I call a fight is only a game, but a witness who saw such a fight in the West Indies agrees with my judgment."

Vipera, Ammodytes, Africana, amoenissima. *1734—35. Hand-colored engraving, from* Locupletissim[um]
Rerum Naturalium Thesauri, *by Albertus Seba. Courtesy O'Shea Gallery, London.*

N°7.

N°2.

N°5.

N°1.

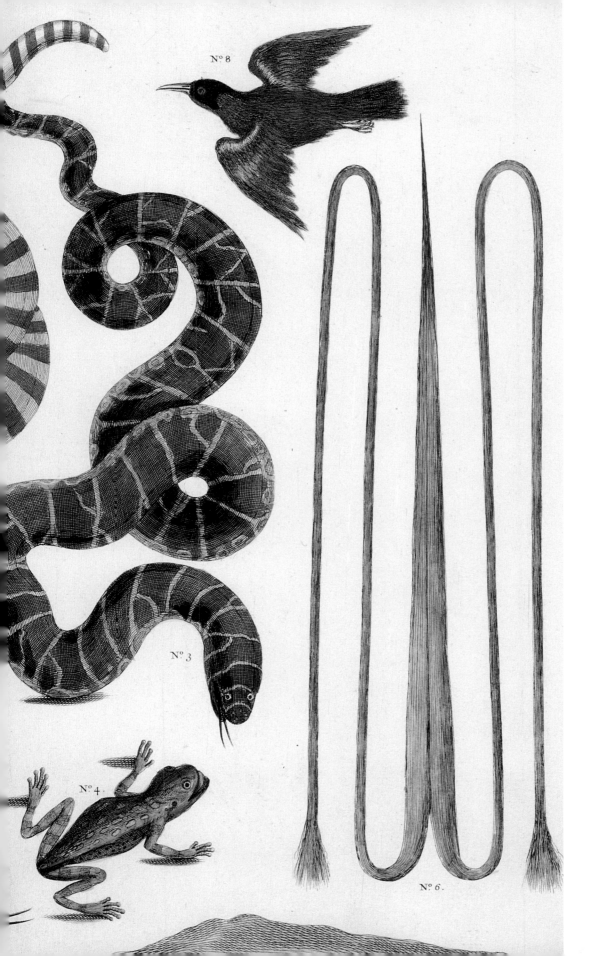

Serpens, marina, Americana *(no.1),* Serpens, marinus, Americanus *(no. 2),* Serpens, marina, Surinamensis *(no. 3). 1734–35. Hand-colored engraving, from* Locupletissimi Rerum Naturalium Thesauri, *by Albertus Seba. Courtesy O'Shea Gallery, London*

*John James Audubon.* Chuck-will's-widow (Caprimulgus carolinensis). *From* The Birds of America, *plate 52. Hand-colored etching and aquatint, engraved by Robert Havell, London, 1827–30. Courtesy W. Graham Arader III, New York*

"The Chuck-will's-widow manifests a strong antipathy toward all snakes, however harmless they may be," Audubon wrote. "Although these birds cannot in any way injure the snakes, they alight near them on all occasions, and try to frighten them away, by opening their prodigious mouth and emitting a strong hissing murmur." Audubon identified the snake between the birds as a "quite harmless" Harlequin snake. In fact, it is a deadly coral snake.

Opposite:
*John James Audubon.* Brown Thrasher (Toxostoma rufum). *From* The Birds of America, *plate 116. Hand-colored etching and aquatint, engraved by Robert Havell, London, 1827–30. Courtesy W. Graham Arader III, New York*

Audubon wrote a text to accompany this study: "Reader look attentively at the plate before you, and say if such a scene as that which I have attempted to portray, is not calculated to excite the compassion of any one who is an admirer of woodland melody, or who sympathizes with the courageous spirit which the male bird shews, as he defends his nest, and exerts all his powers to extricate his beloved mate from the coils of the vile snake which has already nearly deprived her of life." Although the thrashers lost their nest and their eggs, the blacksnake was eventually driven off. Audubon writes that he took the weakened female into his hands, whereupon "she recovered in some degree, and I restored her to her anxious mate."

*Ferruginous Thrush*

TURDUS RUFUS, Linn.

*Male, 1. Female, 2.*

*Black gull Oak. Quercus nigra.*
*Black Snake.*

Drawn from Nature by J.J. Audubon F.R.S. F.L.S.

Engraved Printed & Coloured by R. Havell, London.

Trigonocephalus piscivorous. *Hand-colored lithograph, from* North American Herpetology or, A Description of the Reptiles Inhabiting the United States, *vol. 3, plate 7, by John Edwards Holbrook, Philadelphia, 1842. Rare Books and Manuscript Division, The New York Public Library, Astor, Lenox and Tilden Foundations*

Commonly called the water viper, water moccasin, or cottonmouth, *T. piscivorous* (now identified as *Agkistrodon*) was, according to Holbrook, "the terror of negroes that labour about the rice plantations, where they are more dreaded than the Rattlesnake because the water moccasin attacks everything within reach."

Opposite:
*John H. Richard.* Coluber eximius. *Hand-colored lithograph, from* North American Herpetology or, A Description of the Reptiles Inhabiting the United States, *vol. 3, plate 15, by John Edwards Holbrook, Philadelphia, 1842. Rare Books and Manuscript Division, The New York Public Library, Astor, Lenox and Tilden Foundations*

The house, or milk, snake is a nonvenomous member of the Colubridae family, common to the northern United States. Holbrook wrote that it was gentle in its habits, eating field mice and insects. Because it approached the habitations of men without fear, it was called a house snake. The serpent also frequented dairies and cellars where milk was kept. From the mistaken notion that it robbed dairy women of milk, it acquired its alternate name. *Coluber eximius* is now called *Lampropeltis triangulum triangulum,* the Eastern milk snake.

Coluber eximius.

Plate 3.

# NAJA TRIPUDIANS.

*Bansbunniah keautiah.*
*From life*
*Length 4.3 circum 4"*

Opposite:

*Annoda Prosad Bagchee.* Naja Tripudians.
*Chromolithograph by Hanhart, from*
The Thanatophidia of India, *plate 3,*
*by Sir Joseph Fayrer. London, 1874. General*
*Research Division, The New York Public*
*Library, Astor, Lenox and Tilden Foundations*

Fayrer was a professor of surgery
at the Calcutta Medical College whose
magisterial work was illustrated with
drawings from life by Indian students
at the Calcutta School of Art. Fayrer
was alarmed by reports that at least
20,000 people in India died each year
from snakebite; his book contains a
description of all the venomous snakes
of the subcontinent, an evaluation of
their poison, and a list of remedies.

*Peter Smit.* Python curtus. *Engraving from*
The Proceedings of the Zoological Society
of London, 1889, *plate 45. American*
*Museum of Natural History, New York*

Peter Smit del. et lith.

Mintern Bros. imp.

PYTHON CURTUS

# THE JEWELED SERPENT

---

T he beauty and fluidity of the serpentine form, coupled with its symbolic associations, have made the snake one of the most enduring motifs in the history of jewelry. A Minoan earring in the form of a double-headed serpent survives from the
seventeenth century BC. Assyrian snake-head bracelets and Egyptian bangles with snakes
at each terminal were popular a thousand years later. Statues of Aphrodite were frequently decorated with snake bangles on the left arm, next to the heart. Hellenistic and Roman
jewelers turned out a profusion of ornaments in snake form to satisfy the aesthetic and
superstitious needs of their clients.

With the spread of Christianity, snakes became taboo in the West. It was unthinkable
for a woman to adorn her body with an image associated with the Devil. Snake jewelry
evoked disagreeable, if not indecent, memories of Eve and the serpent in the garden.

The taboo persisted for more than fifteen hundred years, but, by the late eighteenth
century, the power of Christian orthodoxy had waned. Artists and jewelers were inspired
by secular and pagan sources as they rediscovered the artifacts of the ancient world. The
snake with tail in mouth—representing eternity, as it had in ancient Greece—appeared
repeatedly in the sentimental jewelry popular during the early nineteenth century.

Among the opulent pieces of this period were serpent necklaces or bracelets made of
hinged enamel segments, set with precious stones, and sprung so that the bracelet could
wrap around the wrist, staying in place without a clasp. Alternatively, the snake's body was
formed of flexible gold links, suggesting reptilian scales. Sometimes the head was pavé-set
with turquoise stones and cabochon ruby or garnet eyes. Frequently the articulated body
was set with turquoise as well. The art of the jeweler overwhelmed the repugnance people had for reptiles while acknowledging serpents' eternal potency and mystery. Somehow
these Victorian jewels managed to be serpentine without being snakes.

In 1837, at the opening of her first Parliament, Queen Victoria wore a coiled-snake
bracelet made of diamonds with ruby eyes. She treasured a coiled gold snake engagement
ring, a gift from her beloved Albert. Her contemporaries emulated her by wearing twined
golden serpents around their necks and coiled snakes, a favorite motif in Roman jewelry,
around their wrists.

*René Lalique. Snake brooch.*
*c. 1898–99. Gold and enamel,*
*8⅛ x 5¾". Calouste Gulbenkian*
*Museum, Lisbon*

Europe's passion for archaeology and ancient design reached its peak in the second half of the nineteenth century. Italian art jewelers like Giuliano and Castellani established branches in London to capitalize on the craze for classical styles. Their countryman, Benedetto Pistrucci, who had moved to London after the Napoleonic Wars, served as chief engraver for the British Mint from 1817 until 1849. Among jewelers, Pistrucci was known as an elegant carver of high-relief cameos, among them portraits of Roman emperors and the monstrous Gorgon Medusa.

Medusa has had a long history in jewelry. Because her living face was too horrible to look upon, she was most often portrayed in ancient art as a severed head. She was incorporated into Athena's aegis, and people wore amulets and pendants bearing her image to avert the "evil eye."

Medusa was due for a revival in an age intrigued by snakes, ancient deities, and powerful women. Many diadems, collars, brooches, pendants, and belt buckles contained her image. Claude Quiguer, a French cultural historian, has written, "The truly great jewel of 1900 is a tragic jewel, evil and barbarous, in which Medusa reigns with terrible opal eyes."

Art Nouveau jewelers loved images of romantic and scandalous women from the past. They were inspired by nature, especially in its bizarre aspects. They created a fantastic and grotesque menagerie: chimeras, dragons, owls, lizards, beetles, and, above all, snakes. In the workshops of Belle Epoque jewelers, the snake, shimmering and scaly, reclaimed its mesmerizing splendor.

René Lalique (1860–1945), the great French glassmaker and jeweler, was fascinated by snakes. At the Exposition Universelle of 1900 in Paris, Lalique constructed a surreal environment in which to display his art. Black-velvet bats were suspended from a star-filled gray-gauze sky. Below, jewelry was arranged in a vitrine backed by a metal grille of five nude women linked to one another by spidery wings. Among Lalique's exotic creations were a cock's head holding a large yellow diamond in its beak, a butterfly with the head of a woman, and a brooch with ivory nudes surrounded by enameled snakes. His showpiece jewel was a sinister-looking corsage ornament consisting of nine writhing serpents with ropes of pearls hanging from their mouths. The entire array was reflected in a freestanding mirror framed by two six-foot-tall bronze serpents.

Sarah Bernhardt was an early client of Lalique as well as other renowned Art Nouveau artists and jewelers. A flamboyant and unconventional personality, Bernhardt understood the shock value—the simultaneous appeal and repulsion—of reptile jewelry. She once wore a live chameleon attached to a gold chain on her shoulder.

The actress inspired what many consider the most famous jewel of the Art Nouveau period—an elaborate snake bangle and ring joined by a chain. Designed in 1899 by decorative artist Alphonse Mucha and executed by jeweler Georges Fouquet, the piece was the first collaboration between these two Art Nouveau masters. Mucha was Bernhardt's protégé; since 1894 he had overseen the design of all her productions, creating sets, costumes, hairstyles, and jewels. He also designed her publicity posters, depicting her as a typical fin-de-siècle femme fatale—her slim and sinuous body draped in diaphanous robes, her hair unbound in flowing serpentine coils.

In his conception of the jewel, Mucha acknowledged Bernhardt's interest in Eastern objects and symbolism by using curvilinear and crescent patterns derived from Byzantine jewelry. He based the shape of the coiled serpent on ancient gold snake bangles from the late Egyptian and Hellenistic periods and the overall form of adjoined ring and bangle on Indian marriage ornaments popular in the nineteenth century.

The designer, the jeweler, and the actress all understood and capitalized on the serpent's association with sexuality and passionate femininity, as well as on its darker, sinister side. Mucha was also making implicit reference to two of Bernhardt's most famous characters, Cleopatra and Medea (the scorned wife from Colchis whom some legends identify as the priestess of a snake cult), as well as to her title role in *Iseyl,* a play set in ancient India.

Fin-de-siècle gossips reported that Bernhardt had trouble paying for the jewel and that Fouquet sent a messenger to the theater each night to pick up an installment. Still, she held on to the piece until 1908, when she sold it to pay off her son's gambling debts.

*Isaac Snowman.* Queen Alexandra.
*c. 1901. Oil on canvas, 53 x 37".*
*Courtesy Wartski, London*

During her many years as Princess of Wales, and then queen, Alexandra was seldom seen in public without her favorite serpent bangle.

*Bracelets. Egyptian. c. 940 BC. Gold, inlaid with lapis lazuli and blue glass, 1⅓" high. Inscribed for Prince Nemareth, son of Sheshonq I, founder of the Twenty-second Dynasty. The British Museum, London*

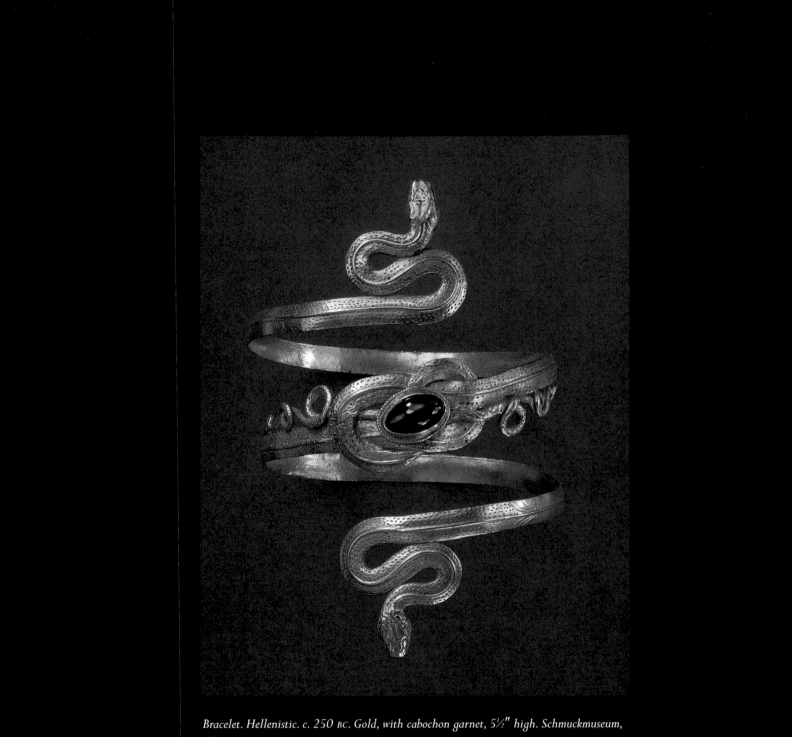

*Bracelet. Hellenistic. c. 250 BC. Gold, with cabochon garnet, 5½" high. Schmuckmuseum, Pforzheim, Germany*

*Medusa head pendant. French. c. 1899. Gold and enamel, 2 x 1⅕". By Courtesy of the Board of Trustees of the Victoria & Albert Museum, London*

Opposite:

*Medusa brooches and pendants. European. Nineteenth century.* Clockwise from top left: *Onyx cameo in a white and gold enamel frame. Onyx cameo, signed by Luigi Rosi. Mosaic, in gold mount, by Castellani. Sardonyx cameo, in silver mounting, signed by Pistrucci, c. 1820. Jasper cameo, in a gold mount with enamel wings and serpents; cameo by Pistrucci, c. 1820, mount c. 1860–70.* Center: *Garnet cameo, with gold and enamel brooch, set with diamonds and emeralds. Average diameter c. 1½".Private collection*

Nineteenth-century jewelers were inspired by Roman images of Medusa. They often added delicate swans' wings to her tangled curls as a reminder that she was a great beauty before she became a Gorgon.

*Nadar. Portrait of Sarah Bernhardt. n.d.*

Right:

*Alphonse Mucha. Sarah Bernhardt as Medea. 1898.
Poster. Bibliothèque des Arts Décoratifs, Paris*

Opposite:

*Hand ornament consisting of bangle and ring joined by fine
double chain. French, designed by Alphonse Mucha, executed by
Georges Fouquet for Sarah Bernhardt. 1899. Gold, enamel, opal,
and diamond. Courtesy Christie's, Geneva*

*Bracelet. English, by Castellani from a design by Michelangelo Caetani. c. 1865. Granulated gold with rubies and emeralds. Schmuckmuseum, Pforzheim, Germany*

*Bracelet. English. c. 1860. Gold and Bohemian garnets, with cabochon garnet. Courtesy Janet Mavec & Co., New York*

*Necklace. Swiss. c. 1840. Articulated gold, enamel with ruby eyes. Donohoe, London*

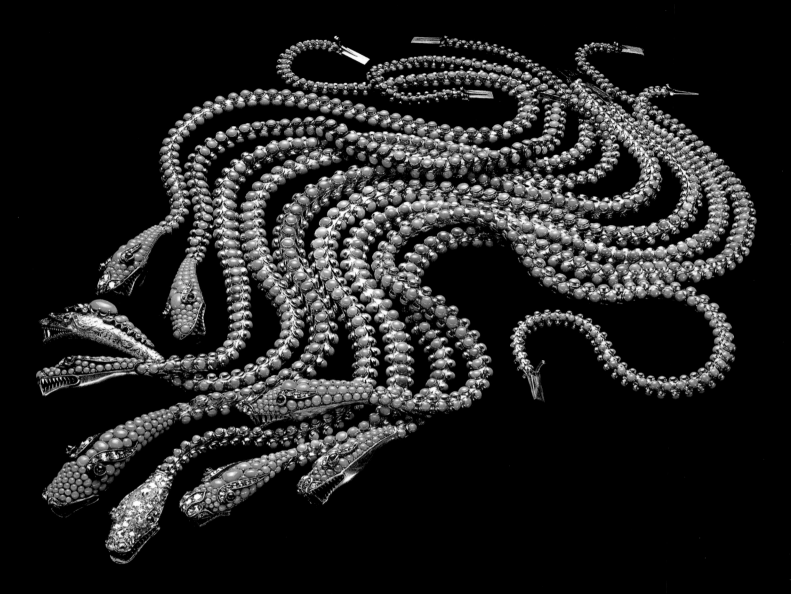

*Necklaces. English. c. 1845–65. Turquoise and gold, with diamonds and cabochon rubies, 14 to 16″ long. A La Vieille Russie, New York*

Opposite:

*Bracelet. English. c. 1845–65. Turquoise on gold with diamonds and cabochon rubies. Private collection*

The turquoise ball hanging from the snake's mouth appeared frequently in Victorian jewelry. The ball was said to represent the world. Alternatively, some snake jewels had heart- or egg-shaped pendants, representing devotion or renewal.

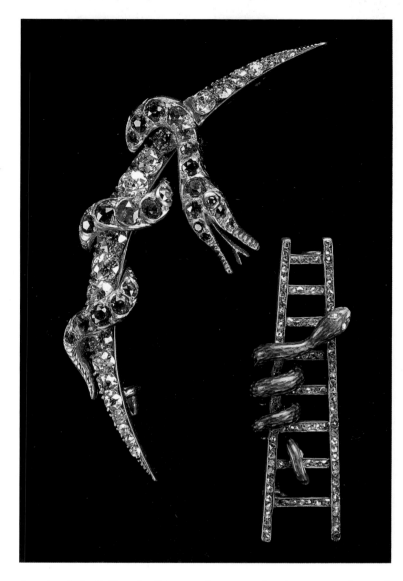

*Brooches.* Left: *Gold snake of demantoid garnets with ruby eye wrapped around gold and diamond half-moon. English. Late nineteenth century.* Right: *Snake of green enamel on gold climbing a gold and diamond ladder. Late nineteenth century. Private collection*

Opposite:
*Necklace. French, by Cartier. 1969. Articulated gold serpent, set with diamonds and lined with red, green, and black enamel. Courtesy Cartier Collection, Geneva*

This piece, and the bracelet on page 125, were part of the collection assembled by Maria Felix, a well-known actress in the 1930s, who was fascinated by snake jewelry.

Below left: *Bracelet with watch. Italian, by Bulgari. Guilloche enamel on gold with diamonds and rubies. 1970–74.*
Below right: *Bracelet. English. Enamel on gold with diamonds and emeralds. 1850–60. Private collection*

Opposite:
*Necklace. American, by Carvin French. Gold and canary diamond necklace with buff-top cabochon rubies and emerald eyes, and gold and canary diamond pendant with emerald. 1990. Courtesy R. Esmerian, New York*

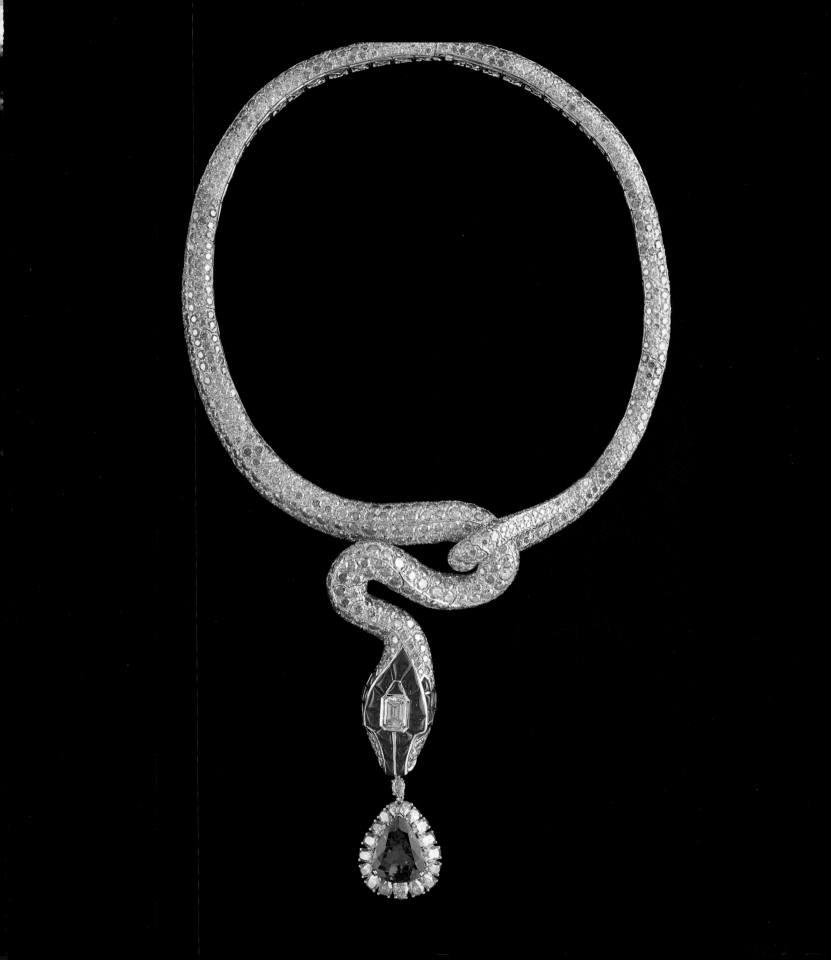

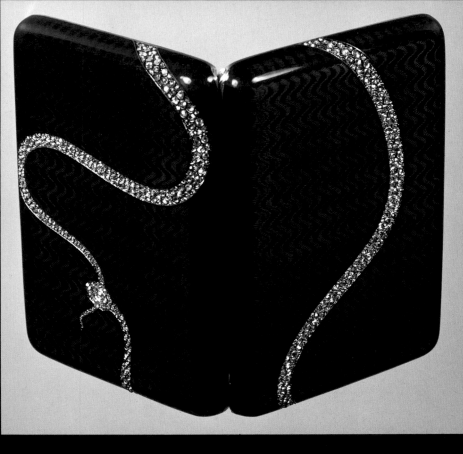

*Cigarette case. Russian, by workmaster August Holmstrom, for Fabergé. Before 1899. Royal-blue guilloche enamel on red gold, encircled by an inlaid snake composed of rose diamonds set as scales in pale green gold. An elliptical diamond forms the push-piece. 3¹¹⁄₁₆" high. The Royal Collection*

This case was given to Edward VII by his longtime mistress, Mrs. George Keppel. After the king's death, Queen Alexandra returned it to the donor as a keepsake. In 1936, Mrs. Keppel gave it to Queen Mary to place in the Fabergé collection at Sandringham. A note, in Queen Mary's hand, setting out this history, is kept inside the case.

Opposite:
*René Lalique. Glass with plique-à-jour enamel, natural pearl, and gold pendant. 1903–5. Private collection*

# SNAKE CHARM

―――――――――――――――――

Edgar Brandt (1880–1960), the French metalworker, is counted among the greatest craftsmen of the twentieth century. His most admired designs include the serpent lamp, which he made in several versions. A cobra, rising from a basket, is the column of the lamp. The snake's head wraps around the glass shade. The object is beautiful and shocking: beautiful because Brandt has captured in gilded bronze the sinuous power of a cobra's body and its shimmering scales; shocking because a creature of the shadows has been transformed into an object that lights a room.

Artists have always been inspired by serpentine forms. Ancient artisans, for whom snakes had religious and symbolic significance, often created pottery and ornamental objects that emphasized their aesthetic appeal. In more recent times, the religious implications of the snake have diminished. Two hundred years ago, an English silversmith designed a Rococo urn with handles formed by the bodies of undulating serpents. Fabergé's workshops turned out snakes made from metal or semiprecious materials to amuse an aristocratic clientele. As the Brandt lamp demonstrates, however, even a secularized representation of a snake has uncanny power.

More than any other modern designer, René Lalique exploited the power of the snake motif in the decorative arts. During the years when he was known primarily as a creator of Art Nouveau jewelry, Lalique also experimented with serpent forms on glass vases and perfume bottles. After 1900 he worked almost exclusively in glass. His workshops turned out inkwells, sugar bowls, flacons, and vases ornamented with snakes. Lalique's serpents writhe; they roil; their jaws gape; they bare their fangs. In the design of his famous "Serpent" vase, Lalique took an innovative, even revolutionary, step forward: the coiled snake is both the decoration and the form of the vessel itself. The snake *is* the vase.

Just after the turn of the century, Lalique created a suede and silk handbag with a clasp of silver snake heads, reputedly for Sarah Bernhardt. Lalique's bag was meant to be audacious, capitalizing on the emotionally charged association of snakes and women.

The relationship between snakes and women has always had sexual implications. Fertility goddesses were accompanied by snakes. The knowledge of good and evil that Eve

*René Lalique. "Serpent" vase. 1920s.*
*Glass, 10¼" high. Courtesy*
*Nicholas M. Dawes*

*Ornamental snake head. Hopewell, Ohio. 100 BC–AD 200. Copper, 20" long. Field Museum of Natural History, Chicago*

Copper deposits of an almost pure form were found in the upper Great Lakes region and traded throughout the Middle West. Nuggets were hammered into sheets, which could be worked paper thin and then incised with stone tools.

acquired after her encounter with the serpent included an awareness of her body and its erotic potential. The Renaissance, in its reappraisal of pagan themes, resurrected ancient femmes fatales like Medusa and Cleopatra, whom legend associated with snakes.

Cleopatra was the quintessential seductress in the minds of nineteenth-century poets and artists. In works by writers like Aleksandr Pushkin, Théophile Gautier, H. Rider Haggard, and composer Jules Massenet, men willingly paid with their lives to spend one night in her arms. Her death by asp bite appealed to both the sentimental and salacious tastes of the age. In numerous paintings and sculptures, the doomed queen languished on a mound of pillows like an odalisque in a seraglio, with the snake slithering toward her naked breast. The historical Cleopatra—a sophisticated Hellenistic matron—was subsumed by the erotic and exotic elements of her myth.

Franz von Stuck (1863–1928), one of the founders of the Munich Secession, specialized in voluptuous paintings of women: Salome, various saints, and a mysterious figure nuzzled by an enormous snake, who is identified only as Sensuality or Sin. She is the eternal female who represents carnal temptation and leads to the destruction of men. And her relationship with the snake is a reminder of the Old Testament, even if there are no overt references to Eve and the garden.

During the late nineteenth century, snake enchantresses had a role in popular entertainment as well as high art. Taking over a speciality that previously had been dominated by men, female snake handlers became a draw for circus sideshows. In an era when the ideal woman was meant to be modest and docile, a scantily dressed young lady toying with deadly reptiles was a titillating attraction.

Female snake charmers were reputed to have exotic origins. Posters and rotogravure handbills announced the coming appearance of a sideshow staple—the "Fair Circassian Lady," who had learned her art from ancient sages and practiced her wiles in the sultan's harem. For a time, every traveling circus troupe included a curly-haired, pale-skinned beauty allegedly born in the ancestral home of the Caucasian race. Audience excitement was piqued equally by the suggestion that the lady had been a prisoner of the "terrible Turk" and by the way she casually caressed the boas, anacondas, and rattlesnakes in her act.

Cirque Molier, which featured a female snake charmer, was popular in Paris during the first decade of the twentieth century. It may have influenced the French painter Henri Rousseau (1844–1910) in his conception of *The Snake Charmer*. Rousseau was captivated by the account of a trip to the tropics taken by the mother of his fellow painter Robert Delaunay. In 1907, Madame Delaunay commissioned Rousseau's haunting evocation of a kind of Eden in which a nude flute player entices snakes to leave the jungle canopy and dance in the moonlight. The flute player, though naked, is not sexually provocative, and the snakes are nonthreatening. Yet behind Rousseau's peaceful dreamworld stretch centuries of associations: There is always a snake in Eden to remind us that human destiny is determined by temptation, sex, death, and the wish for immortality.

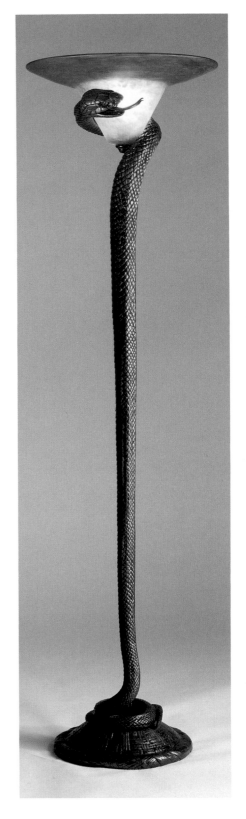

*Edgar Brandt. La Tentation. 1920s. Gilt bronze and alabaster with Daum glass shade, 66″ high. Macklowe Gallery & Modernism, New York*

*Objet de fantaisie. Russian, by workmaster Johan Viktor Aarne, for Fabergé. c. 1900. Silver serpent on turquoise matrix, 7¾" wide. Courtesy Wartski, London*

Opposite:
*Paul de Lamerie. Footed cup and cover. 1737. Silver, 14½" high, 6½" in diameter. The Nelson-Atkins Museum of Art, Kansas City. Gift of Mr. and Mrs. Joseph S. Atha, 1954*

Monot Père et Fils et Stumpf. 1880. Crystal with copper particles, 2⅞" in diameter. Musée National des Techniques du CNAM, Paris

Opposite, above:
*Magnifying glass. Russian, by workmaster Hjalmar Ramfelt, for Fabergé. c. 1910.*
*Gilded silver, with nephrite handle and ruby eyes. A La Vieille Russie, New York*

Opposite, below:
*Lily-pad dish with snake attacking frog. Russian, by Fabergé. c. 1900. Eosite with black basalt, 7¼" long.*
*A La Vieille Russie, New York*

*Turkey Tolsen Jupurrurla.* Children's Python at Tilpakan. *c. 1980. Acrylic on board, 20 x 15½".*
*South Australia Museum, Adelaide*

Opposite:
*Crooked snakes rug. Navajo. 1900–1915. Hand-spun textile, 48 x 39". Collection of Bob Caparas*

Crooked snakes are common in sand paintings but unusual subjects for Navajo weavings,
because it is believed that harm might come to weavers who include sand-painting images in
their work. The three rattlesnakes are moving toward the white line, which represents the
horizon. The red and black triangles stand for clouds. The markings on the snakes are symbols
of deer tracks, while the stripes at the base of the heads indicate that the snakes are venomous.

Left to right:

*Egg and rattlesnake cane. American. After 1950. Polychromed redwood, nail eyes, metal tongue, 35¾" high, 2½" in diameter; Root snake cane. American. Late nineteenth–early twentieth century. Painted root, nail eyes, 43½" high, 7½" in diameter; Woodpecker and snake cane. American. Probably early twentieth century. Varnished polychromed wood, probably maple, 36½" high, 3" in diameter. Collection George H. Meyer*

Snakes are the most common image in American folk canes—probably because the creature was suggested by the shape of roots and branches or saplings that craftsmen frequently whittled into canes.

*Binding panel, designed and executed by Jean Dunand, for* La Chasse de Kaa (Ka's Hunting), *by Rudyard Kipling. French. 1930. Lacquer-on-metal, enamel, morocco leather, 10 x 8⅜". Collectio Priscilla Juvelis*

Ka, a rock python who saves the life of Mowgli, the boy hero of *The Jungle Book*, is one of the few nonvillainous snakes in literature. More conventionally, Kipling also created Nag and Nagaina, the deadly cobra villains of "Riki Tiki Tavi."

Above:
*Jose A. Cunha. Tea service in the style of Bernard Palissy. c. 1890. Earthenware, 8″ high (teapot). Courtesy Nicholas M. Dawes*

Opposite:
*Snake pitcher. 1885. American, Gorham Manufacturing Co. Silver, 10″ high. Courtesy, Museum of Fine Arts, Boston. Edwin E. Jack Fund*

*René Lalique. Sugar bowl and cover. c. 1903. Glass blown into a silver armature, 8½″ high. Calouste Gulbenkian Museum, Lisbon*

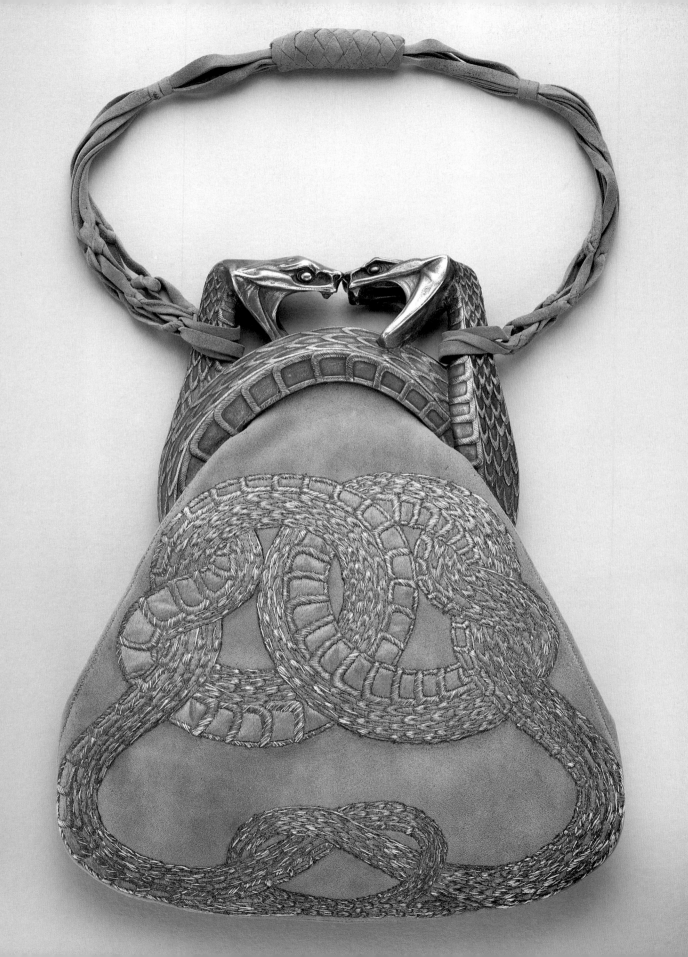

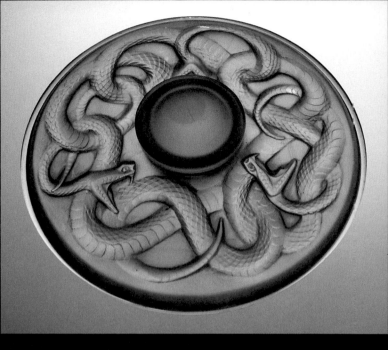

*René Lalique. Serpent inkwell. Designed 1920. Opalescent glass, 5⅛″ in diameter.*
*Courtesy Nicholas M. Dawes*

Opposite:
*René Lalique. Handbag. c. 1901–3. Silk, suede, and silver, 8¾ x 7½″.*
*Signed on upper edge of frame. Private collection*

Two cast and chased silver serpents with gaping jaws form the frame
and clasp of this evening purse; their coils, rendered in gray silk and silver
metallic thread, decorate the gray suede pouch, which may have been
designed for Sarah Bernhardt.

JANE
Avril

H. Stern, Paris.

1899

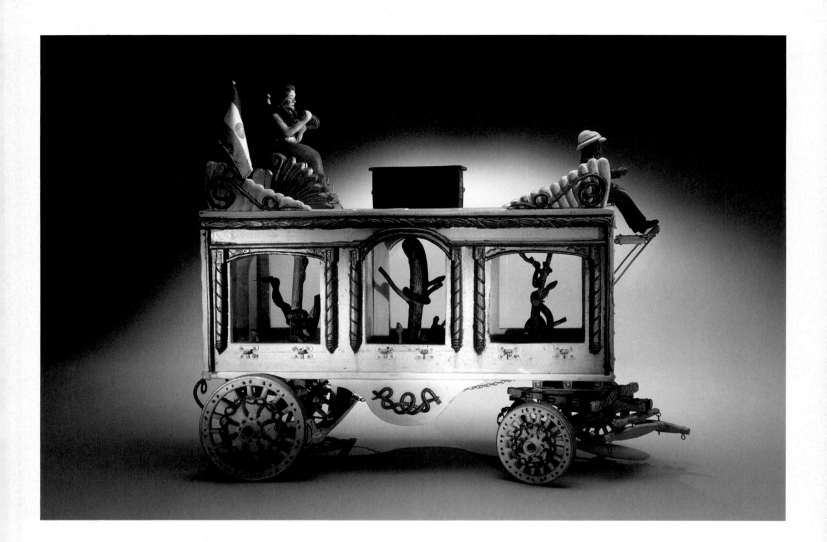

Above:

*Roy F. Arnold.* Madame Orissa. *c. 1925. Polychromed wood, 15 x 41″ overall; wagon: 17½″ long. Shelburne Museum, Vermont*

The lady snake charmer, with one of her charges wrapped around her neck, rides atop Den Cage number 56 of a miniature wagon, drawn by four dappled gray horses. Inside the den are boa constrictors, pythons, cobras, and vipers from Asia, Africa, and South America. *Madame Orissa* is one element of a 300-foot-long wooden circus parade, which includes animals, marching bands, and other sideshow acts.

Opposite:

*Henri de Toulouse-Lautrec.* Jane Avril. *1899. Poster, 56 x 36″. Musée Toulouse-Lautrec, Albi, Tarn, France*

The Fair Circassian Lady. The Original Snake Charmer. *American. Late nineteenth century. Colored lithographic circus poster, 11¾ x 8¾″. Shelburne Museum, Vermont*

NON SINE SOLE
IRIS.

Opposite:

*Marcus Gheeraerts.* The "Rainbow Portrait" of Queen Elizabeth I. *c. 1600. Oil on canvas, 49 x 39". Hatfield House. Courtesy of the Marquis of Salisbury*

The serpent on Elizabeth's sleeve—as well as the heart-shaped stone hanging from its mouth and the celestial sphere above its head—was listed in an inventory of the queen's jewelry made in the year 1600. The serpent may have been an allusion to Athena, the goddess of wisdom, who wore a snake on her helmet. Combined with the heart and the sphere, the serpent implied that Elizabeth's wisdom encompassed both earthly and heavenly matters.

*Piero di Cosimo.* Simonetta Vespucci. *n.d. Oil on panel, 22¼ x 16½". Musée Condé, Chantilly, France*

*Hans Makart.* The Death of Cleopatra.
*1875. Oil on canvas, 74½ x 97½".*
*Staatliche Museen, Kassel, Germany, on
loan from the Federal Republic of Germany*

*Lord Leighton.* The Garden of the Hesperides. *1892. Oil on canvas, 66″ in diameter. The Board of Trustees of the National Museums and Galleries on Merseyside (Walker Art Gallery), England*

According to Greek myth, the Hesperides, "the daughters of evening," guarded the tree with golden apples that Gaia gave to her daughter, Hera. The tree was also protected by the serpent Ladon. Gaining possession of the apples was the eleventh labor set by Zeus for Hercules, who killed Ladon

*Frederick Sandys.* Bhanavar
the Beautiful. *1894.*
*Watercolor and bodycolor over*
*pencil 2 x 7⅓". By Courtesy*
*of the Board of Trustees of the*
*Victoria & Albert Museum,*
*London*

The story of Bhanavar
appeared in a collection
of pseudo-oriental tales by
George Meredith entitled
*The Shaving of Shagpat,*
*An Arabian Entertainment.*
Bhanavar was the beautiful
daughter of a Caucasian
prince. After she gained
possession of a magic
jewel, she turned into an
evil Queen of the Serpents.

*Henri ("Le Douanier") Rousseau.* La Charmeuse de serpents (The Snake Charmer).
*1907. Oil on canvas, 66½ x 74⅜". Musée d'Orsay, Paris. Bequest of Jacques Doucet, 1936*

# Selected Bibliography

*The Anchor Bible Dictionary.* Vol. 5. New York: Doubleday, 1992.

*The Animal Illustrated, 1550–1900: From the Collections of the New York Public Library.* New York: Abrams, 1991.

*The Animal Kingdom.* New York: The Pierpont Morgan Library, 1940–41.

Arader, W. Graham III. *Native Grace: Prints of the New World 1590–1876.* Charlottesville, Va.: Thomasson-Grant, 1988.

Benton, Janetta Rebold. *The Medieval Menagerie.* New York: Abbeville, 1992.

Bevan, Elinor. *Representations of Animals in Sanctuaries of Artemis and Other Olympian Deities,* B.A.R. Series 315. Oxford: Oxford University Press, 1986.

Bogdan, Robert. *Freak Show.* Chicago: University of Chicago Press, 1988.

Boyer, George K. "Significance of the Serpents on Pompeian House Shrines." *American Journal of Archaeology* 46: 1 (1942).

Catesby, Mark. *The Natural History of Carolina, Florida, and the Bahama Islands.* 2d ed. London: C. Marsh, 1754.

Dawes, Nicholas M. *Lalique Glass.* New York: Crown, 1986.

*Dictionary of the Bible.* Edited by James Hastings; rev. ed. by Frederick C. Grant and H. H. Rowley. New York: Scribner's, 1963.

*Encyclopaedia Judaica.* 15 vols. Jerusalem: Keter, 1971.

*Feathered Serpents and Flowering Trees: Reconstructing the Murals of Teotihuacán.* Edited by Kathleen Berrin. San Francisco: The Fine Arts Museum, 1988.

Frick, George Frederick, and Raymond Phineas Stearns. *Mark Catesby: The Colonial Audubon.* Urbana: University of Illinois Press, 1961.

*German Colonial Photography: At the Court of King Njoya.* Washington, D.C.: Smithsonian Institution Press, 1984.

Ginsberg, Louis. *The Legends of the Jews.* 6 vols. Philadelphia: Jewish Publication Society of America, 1954.

Graves, Robert. *Greek Myths.* 2 vols. London: Penguin, 1986.

Holbrook, John Edwards. *North American Herpetology, or A Description of the Reptiles Inhabiting the United States.* Philadelphia: J. Dobson, 1842.

Hovey, M. Oldfield. *The Encircled Serpent: A Study of Serpent Symbolism in All Countries and Ages.* New York: Arthur Richmond, 1955.

Johnson, Buffie. *Lady of the Beasts: Ancient Images of the Goddess and Her Sacred Animals.* San Francisco: Harper and Row, 1981.

Joines, Karen R. *Serpent Symbolism in the Old Testament: A Linguistic, Archeological and Literary Study.* Haddonfield, N.J.: Haddonfield House, 1974.

Kelly, Henry A. "The Metamorphosis of the Eden Serpent During the Middle Ages and Renaissance." *Viator* 2 (1971).

King, James. *William Blake: His Life.* London: Weidenfeld & Nicolson, 1991.

Kinsley, David. *Hindu Goddesses: Visions of the Divine Feminine in the Hindu Religious Tradition.* Berkeley: University of California Press, 1986.

Knappert, Jan. *Indian Mythology.* London: Aquarian Press, 1991.

Koch, Robert. *Hans Baldung Grien: Eve, the Serpent and Death.* Ottowa: National Gallery of Canada for the Corporation of the National Museums of Canada, 1974.

La Barre, Weston. *They Shall Take Up Serpents: Psychology of the Southern Snake-Handling Cult.* Minneapolis: University of Minnesota Press, 1962.

*Lalique: The Glass of René Lalique.* Exhibition catalogue (Magriel Collection). Amherst, Mass.: Mead Art Museum, Amherst College, 1979.

McClinton, Katharine Morrison. *Lalique for Collectors.* New York: Scribner's, 1975.

Meyer, George N. *American Folk Art Canes.* Bloomfield Hills, Mich.: Sandringham Press, 1992.

Mitropoulou, Elpis. *Deities and Heroes in the Form of Snakes.* Athens: Pyli Editions, 1977.

Morris, Craig, and Adriana von Hagen. *Inka Empire.* New York: American Museum of Natural History, 1993.

Morris, Ramona, and Desmond Morris. *Men and Snakes.* New York: McGraw-Hill, 1965.

Munakur, Balaji. *The Cult of the Serpent.* Albany: State University of New York Press, 1983.

Murray, David. *Museums: Their History and Their Use.* Glasgow: James MacLehose and Sons, 1904.

Nadelhoffer, Hans. *Cartier.* New York: Abrams, 1984.

Neumann, Erich. *The Great Mother.* Translated by Ralph Manheim. Bollingen Series, vol. 47. Princeton: Princeton University Press, 1972.

Oliver, James. *Snakes in Fact and Fiction.* New York: Macmillan, 1958.

Padden, R. C. *The Hummingbird and the Hawk.* New York: Harper & Row, 1970.

Parker, H. W. *The Natural History of Snakes.* London: Trustees of the British Museum, 1965.

Parrot, André. *Sumer: The Dawn of Art.* Translated by Stuart Gilbert and James Emmons. New York: Golden Press, 1961.

Payne, Ann. *Medieval Beasts.* London: The British Library, 1990.

Phillips, J. A. *Eve: The History of an Idea.* San Francisco: Harper & Row, 1984.

Randall, Richard H., Jr. *A Cloisters Bestiary.* New York: The Metropolitan Museum of Art, 1960.

Seba, Albertus. *Locupletissimi Rerum Naturalium Thesauri.* 4 vols. Amsterdam: Jansson, Waesberg, 1734–35.

Segal, Sam. *Flowers and Nature.* Amstelveen: Hijnk International, 1990.

Soustelle, Jacques. *Arts of Ancient Mexico.* Translated by Elizabeth Carmichael. New York: Viking Press, 1967.

Topsell, Edward. *History of Four-Footed Beasts, Serpents, and Insects.* London: G. Sawbridge, T. Williams, and T. Johnson, 1658.

# Index

# ACKNOWLEDGMENTS

We are especially grateful for the generous contributions made to this book by Ralph Esmerian, Carole Kismaric, Hugh Nissenson, Marion Fasel, Penny Proddow, Joyce Jonas, and Tom McLaughlin.

We also want to thank the following people who went out of their way to be helpful: Eric Nussbaum, Curator of the Cartier Collection; Darryl Frost and Craig Morris of the American Museum of Natural History; Pauline Mitchell of the Shelburne Museum; Derin Tanyol of Art Resource; Ronnie Brenne of the Bettmann Archive; Joel Kopp of America Hurrah; Peter Shaffer and Rose Casella of A La Vieille Russie; Nicholas M. Dawes; Janet Mavec; Priscilla Juvelis; Lary Matlick at Macklowe Gallery and Modernism; Michael Weisbrod and Elisabeth Porter of Weisbrod Chinese Art Ltd.; Jacqueline Dugas at the Huntington Art Collections; Barbara Hardtwig and Eva Heilmann of the Villa Stuck; David Isaac and Sandy Greenhorn of O'Shea Gallery; Martin Durrant of the Victoria and Albert Museum; Geoffrey Munn and Adam Rattray of Wartski; Ashley Baynton-Williams of Jonathan Potter Ltd.; George H. Meyer; Elisabeth Biondi; Shepherd Raimi; Willard Lustenader; Sharon Valliant; and Aileen Ward.

In our search for images and information, we benefited from the richness of the collections of the New York Public Library as well as from the resources of the Thomas J. Watson Library at The Metropolitan Museum of Art, the library of the Frick Collection, the Pierpont Morgan Library, the Index of Christian Art at Princeton University, and the Yale Center for British Art.

As always, the editors and staff at Harry N. Abrams, Inc., were supportive and enthusiastic: in particular, we thank Paul Gottlieb, Harriet Whelchel, Carol Robson, Barbara Lyons, Neil Ryder Hoos, and Michelle Adams.

# PHOTOGRAPH CREDITS